THE EXCELLENT TRAINER

Dedication

To all the learners and teachers who have played a part in my development as a trainer, whether they know it or not. In particular, those who have encouraged me to look beyond the bounds of what I thought was possible and learn that there is always more to learn.

The Excellent Trainer

Putting NLP to Work

Di Kamp

Gower

Published by
Gower Publishing Limited
Gower House
Croft Road
Aldershot
Hampshire GU11 3HR
England

Gower
Old Post Road
Brookfield
Vermont 05036
USA

British Library Cataloguing in Publication Data

Kamp, Di
    Excellent Trainer: Putting NLP to Work
    I. Title
    658. 312404

    ISBN 0–566–07694–2

Library of Congress Cataloging-in-Publication Data

Kamp, Di. 1949–
        The excellent trainer : putting NLP to work / Di Kamp.
        p.   cm.
        Includes index.
        ISBN 0–566–07694–2 (cloth)
        1. Employee training personnel—Training of—Methodology.
    2. Neurolinguistic programming.   I. Title.
    HF5549.5. T7K257 1996   95–34995
    658.3'12404–dc20   CIP

Typeset in Palatino by Raven Typesetters, Chester and printed in Great Britain by Hartnolls Ltd, Bodmin

BUSINESS

Contents

ing functions; marketing; the design and delivery of training.
The role of the trainer as facilitator and model.

PART V: ACTIVITIES 167

List of Figures

Preface

This book is aimed at those already engaged in training, whether as full-time trainers, training consultants or managers. It assumes an awareness of the principles of training, training methodology and training skills.

The intention of the book is to offer you some alternatives for developing further your existing good practice. Its emphasis is on the trainer as the enabler of learning, rather than as the presenter of facts. This emphasis is in my view more valuable to the trainer in the changing world in which we live, where organizations and individuals are constantly dealing with change rather than stasis.

The book is designed for practical use and includes activities and guidelines which you can use to enhance your practice. The ideas and material are based on neuro-linguistic programming (NLP), which is the study of the structure of excellence. The techniques, approaches and activities it contains are all applications of NLP to the training process.

Di Kamp

Acknowledgements

I would like to acknowledge the particular influence of John Grinder in helping me to find the key to translating NLP back from jargon and complicated activities into common sense and wisdom.

I have appreciated the comments of friends and colleagues who have discussed various parts of this with me. It is always useful to have a different perspective.

I also want to thank John Hume for his patience and invaluable practical help in putting this manuscript together. Without his support, it would have been much more difficult to produce.

DK

Part I

The Context

In order to be excellent we need to be aware of the context in which we are operating. What is excellent in the appropriate context is outrageous in the wrong context. For example, physical movement, shouting and singing are appropriate behaviours at a sporting event or a rock concert, but would have you thrown out of a business meeting.

In this first part we examine the contexts which relate to the excellent trainer:

- the changing world of organizations;
- the changing world of training;
- neuro-linguistic programming.

The first two offer a brief reminder of the implications of the paradigm shifts which have been taking place in the world of work. The introduction of technological innovations is having a profound and far-reaching effect on working practice which has yet to become the norm. Most people are still expecting working life to settle down into familiar patterns and are only just beginning to recognize that the changes are not temporary glitches but a permanent redefinition.

Many of us will have gained our experience of training through traditional routes and will have accepted traditional ways of fulfilling our role. Even if we have recognized the fact that work and training have changed, we will still tend to have models of training which fit better with the industrial rather than the post-industrial age, as we will have been brought up in that tradition.

These traditional training roles and functions are no longer appropriate in the new paradigms. The trainer who is an expert in a particular subject has to add to their skills if they are to continue to be seen as a valuable contributor to the changing world of work. Further, the trainer who can only stand up and deliver a training course as their means of giving information is unlikely to survive the changing demands of organizations for development.

In the first two chapters I will look at some of the reasons for making these statements. The third chapter discusses neuro-linguistic programming. This is the study of the structure of excellence and can give some useful insights into how we can make the differences which will enable us to use our talents appropriately in a changing context.

Excellence is a dynamic quality, always developing, and the techniques and strategies which have been identified provide the basis of the proposals and suggestions for developing excellence as a trainer which form the rest of the book.

1 The Changing World of Organizations

May you live in interesting times. (ancient Chinese curse).

For those of us who are living and working in the closing years of the second millennium, 'interesting times' are here to stay. We are experiencing a period of constant change and the changes are happening at a speed which would have been unthinkable a few decades ago.

We have all been affected by the changes in our everyday life. It is now taken for granted that we can receive information about what is happening on the other side of the world within seconds of the occurrence. Automatic cash dispensers allow us to suit ourselves when obtaining our cash rather than fitting in with bank opening hours. More families than ever use a computer. Meals can be cooked in minutes in microwave ovens.

These examples show that people can adapt to changes and appreciate the benefits which they can bring. They have all appeared in the last few decades and moved quickly from being unusual to being taken for granted.

In the world of work even more technological change has been occurring and with it the need to adapt. Warnings of our need to change our way of thinking about the world of work have been given for quite some time.

Charles Handy said, in 1976,

> Changing values in the environment linked to a changing technology will affect current assumptions of what makes organisational sense. What has appeared to be true for ever may turn out to be only partially true. When that happens change is discontinuous and disconcerting. You can then no longer run tomorrow's organisations on yesterday's assumptions (*Understanding Organisations*, Penguin, p. 411).

In a similar vein John Naisbitt concluded, in 1984, that:

3

Those who are willing to handle the ambiguity of this in-between period and to anticipate the new era will be a quantum leap ahead of those who hold on to the past (*Megatrends*, Macdonald & Co., p. 249).

And Tom Peters has continued to offer reminders and practical strategies to organizations, often radically rethinking his proposals as he has observed the ways in which organizations have succeeded and failed as the changes have taken hold.

Despite the warnings and exhortations, most organizations have lagged far behind the theory in the way they have been working. In my experience there is still much work to be done to enable organizations to catch up with the demands of the changing world of work, and trainers can play an important part in helping organizations to make the transition. However, there are signs that movement is beginning, and we need to be aware of the bigger picture if we are to be effective in helping to make the difference.

I want to challenge you to recognize the significance of the changes and to be aware of the implications for your working future.

All trainers work directly or indirectly with organizations. You may be employed by an organization or be an independent who works with company employees or you may even train through public seminars. Whichever category you fit into, you are dealing with people who live and work in the changing world of organizations and you need to be aware of how these changes are showing themselves, how that affects the people involved and the effect on what is expected of you.

For many, the changes in how organizations work have been traumatic, and there has been significant resistance to them. Yet there is a gradual recognition of the potential excitement of a different way of working. People need help in adjusting to the different working environment, not just in terms of how they act but also in terms of what they expect of themselves and others in the workplace. Where these difficulties are dealt with successfully, a very different type of workplace emerges.

What are these differences?

The dynamic organization

Traditionally organizations have aimed for a niche which would optimize their potential. 'Find the right product, the right market, the right process and the right staff, and you will be successful.'

In today's constantly changing business environment, a niche is at best a temporary resting place. There is now global competition, constant development of processes and frequent changes in demand. Well-known companies have gone out of business because they have relied on past reputation rather than planned for the future. As Tom Peters said in *Thriving on Chaos* in 1988: 'The old saw "If it ain't broke, don't fix it" needs revision. I propose: "If it ain't broke, you just haven't looked hard enough." Fix it anyway' (Macmillan, p. 3).

The successful organization is on a continuous evolutionary path. Its aim is to be always searching for improvement and difference. If a company is standing still it is like someone going the wrong way on a moving pavement – it is effectively going backwards. The emphasis has shifted from finding the right destination to finding the best way of travelling.

The effective organization

Traditionally organizations have had a hierarchical structure which has provided employees with the possibility of rewards and status. Movement up the hierarchy has often been based on qualifications and length of service, and the rationale for supervisory and managerial posts has been that people have always needed to be supervised and managed and there are necessary procedures and stages to any process which have to be enforced.

Often prompted by economic necessity – many organizations could not have survived without reducing their workforce – the slimmed-down organization has now become the norm. For those who are still holding on to the past, this is a disastrous change. Career development seems to have been stopped when there are no longer the various levels of promotion available, and workload simply seems to have been increased as fewer people are expected to be more productive.

Yet it soon becomes apparent that the flatter organizational structures can be more efficient. There is more direct communication with less control and if people are allowed to use their initiative they soon find ways of managing their workload more effectively.

In successful organizations the flatter structure is adding value, both in business terms, and in terms of giving more recognition to the ability of the individual staff. Within these organizations, responsibility for results is being given to those who have to produce the results. What is more they are being encouraged constantly to find better ways of producing the results rather than sticking to 'custom and practice'. Managers are responsible for enabling employees to achieve results effectively, rather than supervising their every move. Again, the emphasis has shifted from 'doing things the way we do them' to 'finding the best way to get the results we want'.

The resourceful organization

Traditionally organizations have acquired resources for a particular purpose and continued to use them for that purpose. This applies to equipment, procedures and employees. This has limited the use of resources and therefore the potential of both individuals and the organization. Now, successful organizations are looking for the fullest use of their resources to increase effectiveness.

When computer systems were first being introduced into organizations, they were for a specific purpose and not considered for other purposes. They therefore frequently were seen as an additional burden, rather than a useful resource. Now the question has become, 'What else can we use the system for?', and technology consultants are being asked to design complete interrelated systems and software packages to expand the usefulness as far as possible.

Linked to this is the whole area of business process re-engineering. The concept behind this phrase is that procedures be designed to facilitate the effectiveness of the organization rather than accepted as a limiting factor.

The third important shift in resourcefulness of organizations is the recognition that people are an asset, capable of adding more value to the organization than any of its other assets. Until relatively recently most people have accepted the limitations of their job rather than used their personal skills and qualifications to the full in their work. They have not been asked what they could contribute, they have been asked if they can fulfil a job description. This produces minimum required, rather than optimum, results.

Most secretaries could give you a list of ways that they could improve the efficiency of their work, but they have been expected merely to get on with the job and can often cite examples of making suggestions to their bosses and being told to leave well alone – its not their job to think of different ways of doing things.

And every assembly worker I've ever talked to can tell you a better way of tackling some part of their job, but no one ever asked them. There are also the classic examples of people who show marvellous leadership skills outside work, or significant abilities in design or problem solving, yet are not required to utilize these skills in their job.

Now successful organizations are considering ways of valuing and maximizing their human resources so as to make the best use of this important asset. People are beginning to be assessed for what skills and abilities they have rather than for what they presently do in their job. They are being actively encouraged to use their skills and contribute their ideas on how to improve the efficiency of their work.

An organization now needs to be constantly developing and adapting to changing circumstances, and those changes are in place far more quickly than they used to be. It also needs to concentrate on results rather than procedures, with a willingness to experiment with how constantly to improve effectiveness. Finally, the emphasis on resourcefulness requires bringing out potential rather than imposing limitations.

These changes in organizational approach and working practice are dramatic. This is not fine-tuning of what already exists. It is a paradigm shift. Individuals at every level in organizations need help in recognizing the significance of the change, in changing their beliefs about what working practice is like and what doing their job well means.

The implications for organizations

Although there are more and more people recognizing that working practice has to change, most organizations are still burdened by a history of how they have been in the past. If I reached the position of senior manager by doing what others had done before me, then I naturally believe that the old approaches are best. Just a few influential people holding on to this belief can seriously affect the ability of an organization to change. What is more, the ordinary worker has grown up in a culture which reinforces the belief that work is a necessary evil, that the workplace is where you do what you can to stop others from exploiting you, and that you save your creativity and common sense for outside work. The changes which are now beginning to be demanded of people do not fit easily within this set of beliefs.

It is important to recognize the strength of traditional beliefs and values in the workplace. People don't normally change overnight, and organizations consist of people. And the beliefs and values which have worked reasonably well for the workplace until now are firmly rooted in many aspects of the organization. Examples abound of where job titles and organization structures have been changed and yet people have continued to behave as if they remained the same. As an example, calling managers coaches and reducing their number does not automatically change their way of managing – and frequently results in significantly greater stress levels for them and increased frustration for those who report to them.

There is also still a tendency to call any initiative which may support change in an organization the 'flavour of the month'. What this means is that people will pay lip service to it for a while, on the assumption that it will soon fade away as have so many initiatives in the past. This is an understandable reaction, as their experience has shown them that many of the innovations have had little lasting impact.

Organizations need help in reinforcing and maintaining the paradigm shift. It is not enough to introduce a new strategy and state that this time it's for real. The paradigm shift requires a total change in working policy. As well as putting any new initiatives into this framework, organizations need strategies for helping people to change their beliefs and values about work in order for the shift to take place. This means developing explicit reasons and justifications for the change and designing these to appeal to a variety of viewpoints. There then needs to be some evidence that this change is going to continue to be taken seriously, to enable people to come past their scepticism and doubts.

Alongside all this it is important to remember that often the negative reactions to change are caused by the tendency to 'throw babies out with the bath water'. Organizations need help in identifying what they already have in place which is valuable in the new paradigm, and to give value to that existing strength.

An example of this was the change of National Health Service organizations to Trusts. Because of the strong emphasis on the need to be business oriented, and self-supporting financially, many of those working in the NHS felt that their traditional values of putting the patient first, and offering the best possible care, were being denied.

Change is often interpreted as 'all new', and therefore understandably resisted, rather than being seen as development, taking the best forward into the new paradigm and adding to it.

If these changes to organizations are to happen successfully, then they need help in identifying models of good practice. Until now the models of success have come from a different history, based on the way things have worked in the industrial society .

There are few models of organizations which have successfully made the shift into a future-oriented dynamic mode of working, where dealing with unpredictability is the norm. The obvious conclusion is that it can't work. So selecting models which people can identify with is important. This may require looking outside the workplace to other types of organization, for example the domestic or social organization. Families or groupings of friends are often good examples of working together in a different way to achieve optimum results. They can remind people of the skills and abilities they have which they use in those settings. Such examples also provide evidence that most people are actually very good at adapting to changes and finding new ways of relating.

It may require smaller-scale models, such as teams or even individuals who are offering evidence of the successful results of good practice in the new paradigm. I have yet to come across an organization which does not have pockets of excellent practice even if it is not acknowledged to be so. If you care to notice what makes the difference in a highly effective team, you will usually find that informally they have adopted a different work practice. Sadly this is often masked by the fact that they are making sure that they look as if they are working 'normally' so that they don't get into trouble for breaking the rules!

This 'new' working practice is not something alien to people – it is based on common sense and natural wisdom, and so is bound to exist already to some degree. The difference is that these qualities will be highly valued in the new paradigm, and such working practice will become the norm rather than the exception.

The implications for individuals

As organizations make these changes, the first problem individuals have to deal with is believing that they are genuine and permanent changes to how the workplace operates.

Since the industrial revolution a strong set of beliefs about work has developed, which is well reinforced culturally. Books, television programmes, advertisements, stories told by older relatives when we are young, all propose to us that we will have to adapt to the harsh reality of work when we grow older and continue to remind us that 'this is how it is'.

These handed-on beliefs include:

- work is restrictive to the individual – you have to learn to 'fit in';
- only a few of us will achieve positions of responsibility;
- most workplaces will squeeze out of you all they can get, for the least possible return;
- there are rules about behaviour, ways of working, decision making, how you make your way up the ladder, which do not follow common sense but which must not be broken.

Although the new paradigm in the workplace is not consistent with these beliefs it may still appear to reinforce them. For example, the slimming-down of organizations, and the way that is handled, can be seen as direct evidence of many of these beliefs, and the statement that the organization values its people is received sceptically as evidence to the contrary is given in the redundancies going on.

Similarly the increased individual responsibility and personal initiative which is now being asked for can be interpreted as burdening someone with more work and giving them more rope to hang themselves.

In order to be convinced that the change is genuine, individuals need direct, practical evidence on a personal level. This is relatively simple to provide. Examples of such evidence which have been cited to me are:

- knowing by first name the MD, and having access to him or her;
- a reward scheme for ideas to improve working practice;

- being offered a choice of training opportunities;
- being treated by a manager as an intelligent person and being asked for opinions.

Once convinced that the change is for real, the individual needs to be convinced that the change will benefit him or her. If organizations are really to be dynamic, effective and resourceful, they need to be full of dynamic, effective and resourceful people. This means that they need individuals to 'buy in' to the change and commit themselves to being part of it.

Very often the benefits of the 'new way' are expressed for the organization as a whole but left implicit for the individuals. We need to be told explicitly of ways in which we personally will benefit, which will appeal to us at different levels: some of us prefer practical benefits such as flexible working hours, some respond to philosophical benefits, such as respect for our ideas and the freedom to do our job in the best way we can think of.

When the individual is convinced that the change is genuine and will be of benefit to him or her, then the biggest intellectual obstacles are overcome.

That leaves the last important question to be answered: 'How am I to behave to be part of this change?' When we ask individuals to shift paradigms in other areas of life there is generally some allowance for the transition, and guidance and coaching may be offered if required. For example, most people are not expected to change from child to adult overnight, and there is some guidance on the different attitudes and behaviour required. There is also a variety of models for us to imitate to help us with the transition, both within our families and in our communities.

Similarly, the individuals who are being asked to shift with their organization need help, guidance and support in making that shift. It's all very well to say that they need to be flexible, resourceful, to take responsibility. We all know what those words imply in the abstract, and most of us have some experience of using those qualities in other contexts. What we don't know is what they mean in practice in the work context.

Individuals need parameters for their flexibility and empowerment in the workplace and examples of what exactly is required, otherwise they are likely to fall into one of the two common traps when we make changes:

1. setting themselves tighter limitations on the changes they make than the organization requires, because they don't want to make mistakes;
   or
2. going along with the change with great enthusiasm and unwittingly overstepping the requirements of the organization, resulting in trouble for themselves, and often for the organization, and a renewal of their lack of faith in the reality of the change.

They may also need a transitional phase, where they are gradually inducted into taking more responsibility, being more resourceful, being more flexible.

Implications for trainers

As trainers we need to be aware of, and informed about, the radical changes taking place in organizations. We have the potential to play an important role in helping an organization make the transition into the new paradigm and we need to be able to understand the changes required, their reasons and their implications.

We can provide a valuable perspective on the practical implications of these changes, through our awareness of the likely effects. Our role gives us the opportunity to offer significant support to organizations and individuals within the organizations as they implement the changes. We are, after all, there to provide recognition and development of skills and abilities, and this paradigm shift is dependent on such work.

Remember that we are operating in this changing context and that doing what we have always done may no longer be appropriate, however well it has worked in the past. The best starting point is to examine both our own place in this changing paradigm and how we need to adapt our own working practice to meet the challenge of an unpredictable future.

2 The Changing World of Training

In this chapter we will examine in more detail the implications of the changes in organizations for the field of training. As I said at the end of the last chapter, we need to be aware that we too have a model of what a good trainer is and does which is based on a form of training which is no longer appropriate for the changing paradigm. If we start by challenging our own 'taken-for-granteds' about what we do before we begin to work with others, then we can more effectively help them to make the changes required to suit the new working practice.

In the past the trainer has been someone with a particular area of expertise who has informed and educated others in that area. Whether you were an expert in technological skills or in 'softer' areas like management skills, you were expected to know all the answers and communicate that information accurately to those you trained. This pressure to be the expert still exists for many trainers. Only recently a fellow trainer asked me how I handled running a new programme for the first time: 'Aren't you worried that you might be caught out by an awkward question that you don't know the answer to?' As well as having a good knowledge base you were also expected to be able to design and deliver a programme which would communicate the information effectively.

Training in being a trainer has concentrated on these two areas of skill, giving people a formula for the preparation of training materials and developing their ability to produce a variety of teaching aids. Although obviously useful as a basis for being an effective trainer, this form of training has led in some cases to a rigidity in the approach taken to training others. There are trainers who say, 'I know that is important to you, but I won't be dealing with it till tomorrow afternoon,' because they are sticking to the rigid programme they have carefully planned. And I still feel a twinge of guilt when someone says to me, 'You mean that you don't use OHPs at all in this programme?' despite the fact that I don't find them to be an effective learning aid for the information I am putting across.

As training became more professionalized a system of certification for being a trainer was developed, so trainers had two areas of expertise: their subject area, and training. Although there have been significant changes in the way trainers are trained there is still a tendency to emphasize the teaching rather than the learning side of training.

Those who are training trainers now will tend to be people who were themselves trained or were trainers, some time ago, when the shift was not so obvious. And many practising trainers will have done their training when the emphasis was on proving professionalism rather than on making learning happen.

With the paradigm shift which is happening in organizations, the role and function of the trainer are also changing significantly and we too need new models of how to work effectively within this change. We will have been pushed to some extent to make some changes to our practice, but we still have to come past the accepted history of what being a trainer means.

The challenge of redefining our role and function to meet the changing needs of organizations is one which we can learn from and develop through, using our existing knowledge and wisdom as the foundation for this development. The changes in working practice are creating some important questions about the need for trainers, and we have to recognize these questions and find ways of using our talents and skills which ensure that we continue to offer value within our organizations.

Who is the trainer?

The first significant difference which challenges many of the traditional values about training is that, more and more, line managers are being given the explicit responsibility for training and developing their own staff. Rather than railing against the obvious lack of respect for training expertise that this implies, professional trainers could recognize the reasoning behind this shift and identify what it implies about their role and function. This gives overt recognition to something which has always happened: employees learn more from an effective manager than they do from a training programme, however good it is. This is because the manager can put the learning directly into a relevant context, can demonstrate its application by modelling the good practice, and can give ongoing support and reinforcement in the workplace. It therefore reminds trainers that, to be effective and valued in the changing organizational world, they need more than their traditional expertise. Trainers need to:

- be fully informed of the context in which their training will be applied and to use relevant rather than hypothetical examples and case studies;
- ensure that they 'walk their talk', both personally and by being able to call on models of good practice that participants can refer to;
- adopt a more holistic approach to the practical application of their subject. How can they arrange/provide ongoing support and reinforcement?

As well as having direct implications for how professional trainers undertake the training they provide, this shift also implies that often the trainer will be training people so that they can train others. More and more, specialist training is being used to 'pump-prime' the spread of the message throughout the organization by the line managers.

Obviously not all managers are automatically effective in training others. The trainer therefore has the responsibility of recognizing that they will need help in developing this skill appropriately within their role. The training needs to be designed to include both the message and how to pass the message on to others. That is, the training is in both the subject, and how to help others to learn it.

To be an effective and valued trainer within the changing organizational context, we need to be prepared to help others to enable learning and give value and support to on-the-job training and also to learn what makes such training valuable, and ensure that the training we offer has some of those elements which enhance the effectiveness of the message.

Training for what?

Linked to the change in who does the training is the shift in emphasis on the objectives of training.

Once upon a time training was seen to be inherently a 'good thing', just as formal education was. The purpose, if stated at all, would be as vague as 'to learn the basics of computing'. This assumption that training was automatically valuable did both trainers and training a disservice. It produced a plethora of training courses which had no particular link to business objectives or personal development plans, and encouraged an expansion of the training field as an area in which to get rich quick, with many poor quality courses being offered.

Those trainers who were offering a high-quality service were tarred with the same brush as those who were simply in the field for personal gain. And training as a whole gained a reputation for being a 'jolly' at best or a waste of time at worst.

Objectives for training when specified were primarily in the area of knowing and understanding the subject. These types of objectives for training still exist in some places, perpetuating the myth that training is for people who want to talk about something rather than a practical development tool.

Training plans did exist in most organizations but were based on custom and practice rather than needs assessment. They would consist of a set programme of courses to be undertaken at certain stages in a person's career, which were considered to be what they needed, without reference to what they may already have or what they would consider to be the most relevant training for them.

There are residual versions of this attitude to training in many organizations today, whether in the way training plans are constructed, or in the lack of clear learning objectives, or in the attitude of people who attend training. However, more and more organizations are beginning to question whether this approach to training really gives the added value they need to be an effective organization.

Economic downturns in the 1980s prompted the re-evaluation of organizational structures for greater effectiveness in a changing world. At the same time training tended to be cut back as being a luxury rather than a necessity, because of the way it had been regarded previously.

In the 1990s training has again begun to be given priority, but on a different basis. Training, like everything else in organizations, is expected to demonstrate a positive contribution to results in the workplace.

So it is necessary to re-evaluate the objectives of training. Just learning about the subject is no longer enough to justify training. People need to be able to apply the learning to make a difference in the workplace and to choose the training which will make the difference they want.

Part of a trainer's skill, then, is the ability to identify what outcomes the organization and the individuals actually want from the training, i.e. what changes they expect to notice as a result of the training. This implies a movement from a theoretical objective – knowledge and understanding – to practical objectives – being able to do something more effectively.

We may already well have been designing training which has practical results, but we need to now ensure that it is an explicit part of the agreement for training. Moreover, while the demand for training which produces required changes is beginning to be made explicit, there are still many instances in my experience of clients who express their training needs in vague terms. This requires of us the ability to elicit information from the client to clarify exactly what results they expect to see. They are quite likely to evaluate the usefulness of the training differently, even if they have not expressed clearly how they will decide whether it is useful or not.

For example, a company which asked for training in time management from a reputable training organization seemed quite happy to be given the standard programme offered by this organization, which included a diary/organizer which participants were trained to use. However, the client company decided against using the training organization again because everyone carried organizers round with them but there was no noticeable improvement in their arrival on time for meetings! Both company and training organization were disappointed because neither side had clarified what was wanted. The company knew that they wanted better punctuality for meetings and less time wasted chasing people up. It also wanted its staff to be able to prioritize their workload better. Because someone had said that both those improvements were to do with time management, and because the training organization was known to run good courses on time management, the company training manager assumed that the course would solve the problem and didn't express the results the company wanted. The training organization did what the company asked for, which was their standard basic training course on time management, based on how to use the diary/organizer which they provided. Only after the event did they discover that it wasn't what the company really wanted. They had assumed that the company knew what they offered in this training and did not check if there were specific results required.

It is the responsibility of the trainer to find out what results are wanted and to educate the company in how to express that, if he or she is to continue to play a useful role in the changing workplace context.

Training in what?

Traditionally, training has been expected to offer participants the 'right answer', whether that be a technical skill or a 'soft' skill like time management. An important selling point has been the ability to offer the latest information, the newest solution, or to offer these in simple, easy-to-grasp ways. However, as organizations begin to recognize their requirement for resourceful, dynamic people they also begin to realize that the solutions to their problems need to come from within the organization and be tailor-made to fit their particular context.

This means that increasingly training is being asked to provide two fundamental elements:

1. help in finding tailor-made solutions through adapting the generic training to suit the particular needs of the company;
2. training in processes rather than products: how to solve problems, devise strategies, use information and develop ideas.

For the trainer this is both a curse and a blessing. The case of the time management course just described illustrates the need to start using tailor-made programmes rather than off-the-shelf packages. It also shows the importance of offering training in the underlying concepts and processes so that people can use and adapt the information to suit their own needs rather than have a narrowly defined product as an end result. This means that we have to design our training in a different way and think about new ways of assessing needs.

On the other hand, the demand for these elements in training gives us the opportunity to make our training more useful and relevant than it used to be, so that we can feel that we have actively contributed to the increased effectiveness of the business.

What form of training?

Perhaps the biggest shift of all in the world of training is the transition from training to give information or particular skills, to training to enable learning.

The essence of the dynamic, effective and resourceful organization is its dynamic, effective and resourceful people. This requires a re-education of most people in what is expected of them at work. Most people have come to expect that, once they have learned their specific job skills, they no longer need to learn anything more. Even if they wanted to learn more and expand their skill base in the work context, their organizations, with notable exceptions, were not prepared to support such non-essential training. We were trained if something was wrong or missing – the deficiency model – and the training was designed to bring us up to standard for the job we were doing.

Some training was offered on the proficiency model. If you were already performing well, you could be 'rewarded' by being sent on the exclusive training, which was for the select few and put you ahead of the majority. It's also true to say that there were quite a number of cases where this was not actually special training but, rather, in special locations, or with special privileges and more of a holiday than a significant personal development!

To be effective in a world of constant change and development demands an ability to be constantly learning and developing. It is only recently that concepts such as 'the learning organization' and 'life-long learning for individuals' have come to the fore. These concepts have to be turned into reality by enabling people to view training and development as a positive and vital continuous learning. This is significantly different from traditional views of training which most of us have experienced.

As some companies began to introduce the concept of lifelong learning, and made it possible for employees to develop and gain qualifications which were not purely linked to their immediate job efficiency, they encountered disbelief from the employees and had to find a way to counteract the long-standing belief that work is what you do after learning.

Now, any successful organization will want all their people to engage on a continuous development path, genuinely in the proficiency model. So training has to start by training people in seeing this as a vital component of their work life, and in learning how to be effective, ongoing learners.

Trainers then need to re-evaluate the training offered in the context of its being a learning event. This requires careful consideration of the training methods used and the overall approach taken to enabling learning. It has to be recognized that people learn in many different ways, and that the trainer's role is to facilitate learning in ways which enable the learners to be effective and get results.

Implications

The role of training

If training is to fulfil its potential in the changing organization it has to become a strategic function. The training offered in an organization must be clearly linked to future business needs, and can usefully provide a long-term perspective, helping to provide the resources in the workforce which will be needed to continually develop the business.

Training needs to be proactive rather than reactive. For example, if the business is intending to become ever more customer oriented, then the training function needs to identify what that will require of the workforce and offer those development programmes before the new approach to customers highlights what's missing, rather than wait to hear what people need because it isn't working.

This means that trainers need to know what is happening at the leading edge of business and bring that knowledge into their own organizations. They also need to be able to translate the visions of their business into the implications in terms of practice for the workforce and for themselves as role models.

Trainers as enablers of learning

The trainer is a prime role model for being a learner. He or she will be constantly developing and learning how to offer ever more effective training to others.

This self-development as a trainer will have as an emphasis how to enable learning and development in others, leading to more variety of approach and method in training plans and programmes.

Trainers as development partners

The trainer will work more closely with both organizational clients and actual participants in ensuring that the training produces the required results. He or she will be proactive in ensuring that the organization has clarified the results wanted in the everyday practice, and will also consult with participants on what will enable them to produce these results.

When training is completed the trainer will actively seek evaluation of results in the workplace to help him or her to amend and refine the training to be as effective as possible.

As organizations change, training also needs to change, if it is to fulfil its potential as an important contributing change agent.

Most training departments and training organizations have begun to make some of these changes in response to the organizational changes. However, they also need to shift paradigm, rather than just redefine or adjust parts of what they do, if they are to continue to be valuable.

Training has for many years been identified with the organization, design and implementation of courses, programmes and events. This history is inculcated in both trainers and those who are our clients, and needs to be addressed directly. Unless we clear out the old-style beliefs about training, we will still be unconsciously governed by them.

The redefinition of training to meet changing needs might be: 'the identification and enabling of relevant learning to meet contextual development needs'.

If training takes on a strategic and practical role of enabling learning in a continually developing organization, then it is pivotal in that organization. If it does not, then it becomes a minor resource to be called on only if it can provide an expert knowledge not being resourced from elsewhere, and plays a minimal role in the development of that organization.

Conclusion

Both the world of organizations and the world of training are changing dramatically.

Everyone reading this will be at a different stage in that process of change, both individually and in terms of where his or her organization has got to. Some will only just be starting on the path of recognizing the need for change, others will have read this and said to themselves, 'I already know all this, and I am already doing the things which we're being told we need to do.'

Wherever you are it is useful to remind yourself that this is a time of significant change, and therefore a time to re-examine ways of working, actively looking for new approaches which may help you to be the excellent trainer. To me, neuro-linguistic programming (NLP) offers a particularly appropriate different approach to training for the new organizational world we are now living in.

3 Neuro-linguistic Programming

Having considered briefly the context in which the trainer is working at the turn of the twentieth century, I will now describe the approach which will be used throughout the rest of the book.

Background to neuro-linguistic programming

NLP was first developed in the 1970s by two young men, John Grinder and Richard Bandler, at Santa Cruz University, California. They came from different disciplines: John Grinder was a linguist, Richard Bandler a mathematician and student of psychology.

Together they explored what they had learnt, and what they saw as areas which no one had fully explored yet. To them the most glaring omission in research was what people did right. There were thousands of studies of the dysfunction of individuals and societies, from many different perspectives and disciplines. There did not seem to be any interest in finding out what makes people function well. They felt that this type of information could be far more useful to far more people than the usual areas of research, so they decided to see if they could find out what made someone excellent in their field. They began by studying three outstanding therapists to see if they could find out how they achieved excellence.

To this study they brought their different perspectives and a shared curiosity. They spent time with these people, noticing and asking about the way they thought about things and responded to situations. From this they began to identify certain patterns of communication which seemed to make the difference. This communication was often not consciously chosen by the individuals – it simply was how they thought or acted automatically.

The two men started by trying out these patterns themselves, and found that they seemed to make a positive difference. They then began to give talks and workshops to suggest to others that they try out the patterns, and NLP started to develop further. They had discovered that excellence can be consciously learned rather than remaining as an occasional occurrence for most of us.

Since that time many have studied to learn the patterns, and much more research has been conducted to develop more and more sophisticated material on the patterns of communication which constitute excellence.

A description of neuro-linguistic programming

Grinder and Bandler called the patterns 'neuro-linguistic programming' because that seemed to sum up the essence of what they were discovering.

We communicate about our experience to ourselves and to others through two means:

1. Our neurology, that is, how we 'translate' experience with our brains into our physiology. An example of this would be the way our bodies and facial expressions automatically reflect that we are excited, even though we are trying to act as if we are unaffected.
2. Our language, that is, the specific words and formulae we use to describe something. An example of this would be the difference between saying 'I don't want to learn to drive' and 'I want to learn to fly.'

In addition we learn to react in certain ways to certain specific situations, and develop automatic patterns or 'programmes', both in our neurology and in our linguistics. For example, most of us have, quite unconsciously, an automatic programme for greeting someone we know and like which includes what we say, how we say it, how we move and react physically to them and what our facial expression is like.

These types of programmes constitute most of our daily responses, to ourselves, to others and to our environment, and are variously described as our personality, the way we tick or 'just the way I am'. We do not usually stop to consider these responses unless they cause us significant problems.

However, NLP challenges us to become conscious of the patterns we have. By studying and making explicit the patterns of excellence, NLP researchers have offered a framework for us all to reconsider our own patterns of communication with ourselves and with others. They provide evidence that all the patterns we use unconsciously have actually been learned and developed by us through observation of others and personal experience.

They propose, therefore, that we can, if we want, review our own patterns and take conscious control of them.

NLP shows us how to identify the automatic responses we have so that we are aware of the way we are influencing ourselves to produce certain reactions and behaviours. We can then choose to apply consciously the most useful ones when we want to, so that we are able to call on our own excellence at will rather than hoping that it might appear when we need it. We can also replace the less appropriate ones by learning how to develop our own excellence into automatic programmes and adding in some of the patterns of excellence identified by the NLP researchers.

A simple metaphor for this development is that NLP provides us with the user's manual for the wondrous computer we call our brain so that we can begin to utilize it effectively.

The challenge of NLP

This approach is a powerful challenge to traditional thinking about how human beings become who and how they are.

Human potential

We have been led to believe that we are limited in our capabilities. Whether the limitations are seen as being inherent to us as individuals, or caused by our environment and upbringing, there is nonetheless an accepted view that we have to learn how to live with those limitations.

The NLP approach suggests that anyone can become excellent in their reactions and responses if they are given the tools, and questions the assumption that we have to live with our own particular strengths and weaknesses, and those of others, proposing that we can learn to be good at or successful at anything we choose.

The implication is that when we say we can't do something, we should check whether that means that we don't want to or that we don't yet know how to. And if we want to learn it, then it is always possible.

Although this sounds idealistic, when we stop to consider our own life experience most of us will be able to find an example of this ability to go beyond our apparent inherent weaknesses when we want to. Many unco-ordinated and clumsy people learn to drive well – a skill that requires co-ordination. Many people who can't do maths can calculate darts scores in their head. It is evidence of this kind that it is possible to change that NLP then uses to help us acquire the tools to consciously choose to make more changes.

Finding the resolution

The second way in which NLP directly challenges traditional thinking is through its proposition that we pay attention primarily to the resolution rather than the problem. We have all learnt that problems need to be analysed and discussed, that causes and symptoms need to be explored. Only when we have thoroughly examined all the aspects of the problem we can find will we begin to look for possible solutions.

In studying excellence the founders of NLP discovered that excellent people pay most attention to the desired outcome – how they want things to be – rather than to what's wrong. The problem is merely clarified, rather than explored, and then the ideal resolution is defined in as much detail as possible. From that, they can work out strategies which may help them to achieve the ideal resolution.

Although this idea contradicts custom and practice it none the less makes sense. If we put a lot of energy into analysing a problem we have less left for solving it. What is more, we are giving the problem even more weight by our attention, and therefore making it seem even bigger and more difficult to get out of. Finally, by concentrating on the problem as something to get rid of, we often don't clarify exactly what we may substitute for it – it's no accident that we have the aphorism 'Out of the frying pan into the fire'.

Again, the change of perspective from the problem to the resolution also resonates with some parts of our own experience, because we have all been 'on good form' some of the time. When, for example, our day is generally going fairly well, if one meeting is disastrous we may well respond to that quite positively. Instead of agonizing over what went wrong we may consider how we wanted it to go and even take immediate action to remedy the situation.

Natural learning

The third challenge NLP offers is its proposition that learning comes easily and naturally to human beings, and that we can make changes to ourselves and to what we do without having to try too hard.

NLP points out that, as children, we all learn enormous amounts, apparently without any great effort – language, movement, behaviour, attitudes – so, if we can re-engage with the natural learning ability, we can continue to develop ourselves in ways we choose and become the dynamic creatures we were intended to be.

This conflicts with the assumptions of our formal educational systems which classify our limitations as learners and teach us that learning is difficult and requires great effort as well as some form of innate ability.

Yet the NLP approach is borne out by our own experience that when we are motivated to learn, and when the relevant information is offered to us in a way which suits us, we can all learn easily.

I remember that when I was a student, I wished I could knit so that I could do something productive while we sat around talking in the evenings. My mother, grandmother and various schoolteachers had attempted to teach me, to no avail. A fellow-student volunteered to try to teach me. He started by showing me what to do if I dropped a stitch or went wrong in a pattern so I was less worried about making mistakes. He then taught me to knit by touch, without looking. Within a week, I was a competent knitter, and my third 'production' was a Fair Isle sweater! What made the difference? I had some purpose in learning, and he geared the teaching to my needs and my 'style'. No doubt you have some similar experiences of learning easily and quickly.

To sum up, NLP, by researching how excellence is created by people, has made important challenges to the perceived wisdom of Western culture. Although this may upset the vested interests which are challenged – experts on human nature, teachers, psychiatrists, etc. – the alternative views put forward by NLP do resonate with some part of our individual experience and so have an attraction for people. It would be good to believe that we are able to be how we want to be, and that we could achieve it easily, even if it does disagree with the perceived wisdom.

Once these basic descriptions of the potential of human nature are perceived as attractive, the next step is to ask how we can develop that potential.

NLP is not alone in proposing these principles – they have appeared in many philosophies throughout history and are held up as ideals in a variety of approaches to self-development. What most supporters of such principles have given us is the belief that we can be more than we seem to be and some stories of individuals who are living examples of the potential of the human being. They have then suggested that the way to get there yourself is along exactly the same path these individuals have used: 'If you meditate twice a day, eat fruit and nuts and live in a warm climate with a private income, you will be able to develop your potential too!' These prescriptions for developing our potential will for most of us seem either unattainable from our present state or unattractive to us.

The difference with NLP is that it offers a framework for developing yourself based entirely on how people set themselves up unconsciously when they are being excellent. It spells out the underlying principles which enable people to develop their full potential in whatever context and by whatever specific path.

This provides a universally applicable framework, with room for customizing to suit individual and cultural needs, not an imposed rigid structure which limits possibility rather than extending creative potential.

NLP research has identified the fundamental patterns of excellence, and offers them as a blueprint from which individuals can construct their own unique version. It emphasizes that the essence of excellence is uniqueness.

We all know that when we learn something, and follow the rules, we can be 'good enough' – that is, our performance is as good as, and interchangeable with, that of others. However, someone who is excellent has always added their own personal touch and made that slight adjustment that takes their performance into a different class, whether it be how they make the tennis stroke or how they greet someone.

NLP is not about conformity but how to uncover your own unique way of being excellent. It does not prescribe the way we have to live, act or respond; it helps us to develop the prescription which will best suit us as individuals. This framework is far more attractive to the human spirit than an imposed 'right answer'.

If we are to begin to undertake this, we need to find out how to begin. NLP starts with the most important part of our thought process in any given situation – what we believe and use as our operating principles.

The operating principles of NLP

Every theory to do with human nature implies a set of values and beliefs about human nature. In fact everyone has developed their own set of implicit operating principles which unconsciously guide their actions and reactions. These come partly from our cultures, partly from our upbringing, and we add to or amend them through our own experience. They are usually identifiable when someone says 'That's just how it is' or 'It's obvious', and are usually sweeping statements about how human beings operate and how the world works. For example, 'No one likes a loser' or 'People are basically lazy' or 'You can't always have what you want'.

NLP takes seriously the importance of operating principles in defining what we think is possible in our lives. There is an explicit set of beliefs and operating principles which is clearly stated as the first requirement if you want to be excellent.

Research continues to indicate that excellent people make the assumption that these operating principles are true, and so find evidence that supports them. It is interesting to notice that there is no attempt to claim that they are right, or true, only supporting evidence that they are useful operating principles to live by if you want to be excellent.

The operating principles have been expressed in many different forms. Here is my preferred version of them, with brief explanations of their implications.

We each already have all the resources we need to be wise and excellent

When we act as if this were true we are reminded to look for the best, rather than the worst, in ourselves and in others. We are also prompted to continue to explore until we find the key for tapping into those resources, rather than assuming that we are not capable of being wise or excellent in this situation.

For us as trainers, adopting this operating principle means that we regard all trainees as resourced rather than ignorant or lacking. Our task is to make them aware of their resources.

For example, a group of new graduate intakes who are to be trained in basic management skills may, according to our usual assumptions, be considered totally ignorant of what is required of them in management. Yet they do have relevant experiences which can be tapped into. They have managed relationships with peers, with lecturers, with parents. They have also unconsciously absorbed information about how managers function – in banks, shops and other places of work. As trainers we can tap into this information which they have unconsciously collected and help them to formulate it consciously.

Those who are most flexible have most influence

This principle points to the fact that there is not usually only one right way of responding or reacting.

For trainers, it is a reminder to take notice of ideas and strategies which are different from our own, because they may demonstrate this flexibility. It also prompts us to encourage our trainees to think of a range of alternative strategies so that we are helping them to increase their flexibility. It also encourages us to extend continually our own range of responses and reactions, to cater for the differences in our trainees and so increase the likelihood of our influencing them.

I frequently come across people who have been assessed in some form of psychometric testing and therefore 'know' that they can or can't react in certain ways: 'I am an introvert, so I can't give presentations confidently'. If I am to be influential in helping this person to be confident in presentations, I need to be flexible enough to respond in a way that accepts the statement yet encourages the person to consider the possibility that he or she can still present effectively. So I will agree that they do have introverted aspects of their personality, and also help them look for examples of when they have been extrovert, or how they can use that to help them to present effectively, for example by reminding them of others who present effectively yet are not particularly extrovert.

Everyone makes the best choice available to them at the time

This operating principle is very challenging to our 'normal' way of reacting: we usually make a judgement that concludes that a choice is either right or wrong. This presupposition changes that reaction into an acknowledgement that a person has an appropriate range of choices or needs to develop some more appropriate choices.

The principle's primary application is to ourselves, so that instead of berating ourselves because we reacted inappropriately to a situation, we use our energy to find alternative ways of handling it when something similar occurs again.

When applied to others, it makes us consider whether we can make any difference to the situation which will enable someone to make a more appropriate choice. If a participant has refused to take part in a particular activity, I would previously have castigated myself for presenting the activity badly, or perhaps even for putting it in as part of the programme. Alternatively, I would have considered that person to be awkward or disruptive.

With this presupposition in mind, I take a different tack. I ask myself how I could present the activity in a way which encouraged that person to take part, and what else I could do to make that possible.

There is no such thing as failure, only feedback

When I first came across this operating principle I was sceptical about its usefulness. It sounds like one of those pat phrases which are used by 'positive thinkers'– but our experience demonstrates that there is failure and that we suffer for it. However, I did begin to see its usefulness when linked to the previous operating principle. If something I have done or said has failed to elicit the response I wanted, I now have more information which I can use to prompt me to extend my range of choices.

This operating principle, in fact, has helped me to find the places where I need to develop my skills, and has encouraged me to look deliberately for the challenges which stretch me rather than to play safe.

From that personal experience I have been able to offer this operating principle to others as useful, in terms of how we use it as a spur to our personal development.

Others may still tell us we've failed. However, we can often change that reaction too if we demonstrate we have learnt from it. Consider the manager who decided to run his meetings as an open forum instead of using a set agenda. The same staff who had complained of the restrictions of the agenda approach complained that the unrestricted meeting achieved nothing and just wasted time. The manager did not react defensively, nor did he just revert to the use of a set agenda. At the next meeting he started by talking about the comparative merits and demerits of the two approaches and then proposed a third alternative, with an agenda for part of the meeting and a time allocated for open forum on a particular topic. His staff felt that notice had been taken of their reactions and responded constructively to his proposal. Through this demonstration of having learned from his mistakes the manager enhanced their respect for him.

If what you're doing isn't working, do something different

This operating principle links to the previous three about flexibility, choices and feedback. It seems such an obvious statement, yet we frequently just repeat in the same way if our point hasn't been understood or we haven't had the effect we want. The principle is a reminder that we need flexibility in approach: different ways of saying it, demonstrating it, coaching in it. It can also be interpreted in a wider sense. We all know the feeling of being full of information – those times when we can't absorb any more – and the 'indigestible' feel of something which is difficult to accept. At these times we need to allow time for 'digestion', to continue the analogy. As a trainer I may give people an extra break, or move on to a different, lighter subject, in order to allow for absorption. Later, I can return to the subject and often find that the group is closer to understanding or to the effect I wanted, just because some space was given.

A common phenomenon illustrates the usefulness of this presupposition beautifully. Think of how often, when we are 'stuck' in dealing with something, we have a sudden physical urge to go to the toilet. Remarkably, having satisfied that urge, we are often able to start moving again on our issue! Does this mean that toilets provide significant sources of inspiration? Maybe it is just a natural way of doing something different, giving us the space we need to take the next step.

All behaviour is communication

This operating principle is useful to keep in mind when we say things like 'I didn't say anything,' or 'I didn't do anything!' We cannot *not* communicate. Even when we are on our own, we are communicating with ourselves about our situation, by our physical posture, by the way our thoughts are formulated.

The principle reminds us as trainers to notice everything our trainees are communicating to us, not just their spoken words. We all know that this communication is happening, but often we don't respond to it immediately. We may ask someone if they have grasped the point. They may say yes, yet their facial expression and the way in which they say it suggest that they are still not sure. When later it becomes apparent that they are not yet able to use the information, we say, 'I knew he or she hadn't understood.' In other words, we 'read' the communication, yet we don't respond to it. This operating principle encourages us to respond to the non-verbal communication at the time it happens.

The principle reminds us as trainers to be aware of the messages we are giving out. It is not enough to 'learn the script' of what we want to convey to our trainees. If we are not convinced of its usefulness, they will sense our lack of conviction. If we don't believe they are bright enough to put it into practice, they will feel our condescension.

We have all experienced the technically perfect trainer, teacher or expert who failed to change the way we thought or acted. Remember that our trainees are just as astute as we are at picking up non-verbal communication, whether they know it or not.

The meaning of your communication is the response you get

Linked to the previous operating principle, this one puts responsibility firmly into our own court. It stops us saying: 'You misunderstood' and makes us ask instead, 'How can I express it so that you respond in the way I want you to?'

The principle, yet again, prompts me as a trainer to increase the flexibility of my approach. If someone tells me that the clever strategy I have presented won't work in their environment, and I believe it will, then this operating principle makes me reconsider how I can present the strategy in a way which makes its relevance and usefulness clear to that individual. I am also reminded to check that not only my words, but also my non-verbal communication, are giving the same message. If my body language is conveying the message, 'But you won't appreciate this', then that may well be the communication which is being responded to.

Unless you know what you want, you will not be able to know if you have it

This operating principle is a reminder to consider carefully before we start what outcomes and effects we want. Most of the time we have some idea of what we want, but our thoughts are ill defined or defined in a narrow way.

We may want someone to agree to do something. They do agree, but we are not satisfied because we wanted them to be enthusiastic as well! Or they may not agree, yet we are happy with the encounter because the discussion was lively and their arguments were valid and useful in making us think about the issue in a different way.

As a trainer I use this operating principle to remind me of how I want the trainees to be, as well as what I want them to understand or learn, within the training event. It also makes me aware that I want the training to have an effect in the workplace, and prompts me to ensure that the material I offer can be applied in the workplace context, and to check that it has proven to be useful in that context some time later.

By thinking through what we really want we identify the evidence which will tell us that it's happening. This gives us the yardstick to monitor continuously in the fullest sense whether we are continuing to work towards our outcome, and encourages us to do something different if any part of it is not working as well as it might.

We create the story of our lives

The final few operating principles are all linked to the theme of personal empowerment. This one tells us that it is up to us to choose how we interpret and act on what happens to us. For example, redundancy for one person is a catastrophe, for another is an opportunity to rethink and reshape their lives.

As trainers we can encourage people to interpret events in a constructive way and take responsibility for using everything that happens as an opportunity to learn and develop. By doing this people become more proactive in making their lives constructive and reduce the likelihood of being a victim of circumstance.

For many who apply this operating principle it has a deeper meaning. It proposes that we can actively direct our own 'story' and choose how it develops. This gives them the incentive to use the previous operating principles to help them create a story for their lives which uses their full potential, rather than accepting the limited version which seems to stretch out in front of them. We all admire people who seem to have taken their lives by the scruff of the neck and transformed what is happening to them, whilst wondering how on earth they did it – maybe they just believed they could create the story of their own life!

To be at our most effective, we need to use all of us

This operating principle states that we are not just a rational mind. So often we think things through rationally and ignore the messages from our intuition, our heart and even our body. Yet unless the whole of us is in accord with our action or statement, there is an incongruence which shows through and affects our performance.

Think of the difference in the way you do something because it's sensible and logical and the way you do something you're committed to. We all have people we admire because they 'put so much into what they do'. What we are recognizing with that admiration is the difference it makes when someone behaves in a way which shows that their heart, mind and body all are in accord and involved.

Similarly, this applies to our response to situations. When we respond only through our intellect, we may well be technically correct but our reaction will lack warmth or feeling. Most people prefer someone to be what they call 'genuine'. This usually means that they feel that they have received a heartfelt response rather than a purely intellectual one.

The principle again tells me, as a trainer, that I need to be convinced of my message to be convincing, and that my non-verbal communication is at least as powerful as my verbal communication of the message.

The world is a place of abundance

This operating principle is useful in giving us permission to develop ourselves and others as far as we possibly can, rather than putting a limit on our development. It encourages a frame of mind which says that there is always the potential for more, rather than that there is limited scope and a need to compete within that scope.

The principle can be difficult to accept, particularly in a world where what is brought to our attention is how little there seems to be to go round, whether that be material or emotional. I was educated to compete with others for the scarce resources. If I didn't do well at school, I wouldn't be able to have the good job, financial resource and material goods that only the special few can have. If I wasn't a good girl I wouldn't be loved and cared for, because only some are. And if I didn't watch out others would take from me and I would be left impoverished in some way.

Despite the power of this message of poverty and limitation in our world, there is also plenty of evidence that the opposite can be true, and we need to begin to collect that evidence. Billy Connolly, a Scottish comedian, remarked that we have been told through our media that there is now a state of 'compassion fatigue' in the world – we can only give so much to help others, and then we have to stop because we have run out. As he went on to say, ' If we called it love, would you really think it could run out? Don't be so daft!'

As a trainer this operating principle encourages me to look continually for ways of extending myself, personally and professionally, and to notice what else is possible.

It also enables me to encourage others to go as far as they can in their own development, even if this means that they surpass me in some way. By doing so, through the filter of this operating principle, they are merely leading the way for me to do the same, should I wish to.

Despite the evidence that opportunities are becoming ever more limited, particularly in the workplace, there is equally evidence that collaboration and partnership can lead to expanded possibilities.

When we are attuned to ourselves and the world around us, magic happens

The final operating principle of NLP is a reminder that our moments of inspiration, of genius even, are when we are acting as if all the previous presuppositions are true.

When we are respectful of ourselves and others, then there is a synthesis of our wisdom and excellence which results in quantum leaps.

We have all, as trainers, experienced, those moments of inspiration when we have just said or done the right thing at the right moment to produce a result that is way beyond what we would have achieved if we had stuck to the script. The principle is a reminder of how that can happen and what we can do to make it more likely. What is more, everyone has experienced their own version of those moments of inspiration, and if we can help others to tap into what made that moment so special we will increase the amount of magic happening in the world!

The operating principles of NLP are rather like the Ten Commandments in the Christian Bible. They are a set of precepts which, if we live by them, affect our behaviour, towards ourselves and others quite automatically. However, they do not give us enough information on their own to enable us to be excellent whenever we choose. NLP therefore spells out the elements of our thinking and behaviour which make a difference to our performance, to flesh out the basic skeletal structure provided by the presuppositions.

The common threads of NLP

Each NLP technique or strategy is designed to elicit a particular result. However, there are a set of common threads which are a part of every technique. They are, if you like, the musculature and circulatory system which are vital to the successful working of the particular technique. These common threads are vital to the successful application of the specific techniques. Although they may seem obvious, spelling them out helps us to identify what may be missing when something is not working as well as we thought it would. Further, these common threads, on their own, without being attached to a specific technique, can make a difference to our performance.

Physiology

In NLP our physical state is given prominence in every technique. This is an emphasis which is common and recognizable in sports training but not usually mentioned in other forms of personal development. Yet it is equally important in our everyday performance. How we are standing or sitting, which muscles are relaxed or tense, affects our mental and emotional state. As a simple example, walking briskly with our arms swinging, our head up and a smile on our face is almost guaranteed to dispel a melancholy mood.

To take this further, small yet significant differences in our physiology provide unconscious pointers to how we are mentally and emotionally in particular situations. Our body responds unconsciously to experiences, and then adopts a similar position when we think that we are about to have the same experience. If we take conscious control of this reaction we can put ourselves into a physical state which reminds us of our best experiences and helps to trigger us into similar performances.

Furthermore, our physiology unconsciously calls on responses and reactions from others. So consciously choosing a useful physical state has a positive effect not only on ourselves but also on others. Again, a simple example is the different ways we react to someone who looks cross and someone who is smiling.

This attention to physiology in each technique comes from the study of excellence and the identification of the importance of our unconscious neurological responses and reactions in affecting our performance. It gives us a simple way of making a difference to our performance which would not usually occur to us consciously. What we usually try to do is to 'think' ourselves into a particular frame of mind. That can be hard work, and it may be much easier to physically position ourselves for a different frame of mind. Sometimes our unconscious wisdom does this for us. An everyday example would be when someone unexpectedly demands a high level of attention from us, perhaps by asking us to help them sort out some problem they have. Our initial response is often to suggest that we go somewhere quiet to talk about it. This also gives us the opportunity to adjust our physical state to be ready to pay the appropriate attention.

Language

The second thread running throughout NLP techniques is our use of language in the sense of linguistic formulation, or ways of expressing ourselves.

Again, the way in which we put our thoughts together, to ourselves or to others, can have a significant effect on our performance. 'I hope I don't forget x' introduces that doubt or fear into our consciousness and in fact increases the likelihood of our forgetting. On the other hand, 'I will remember x' is a statement of intent which enhances our likelihood of remembering.

At a more complex level, there are words and phrases which are clearly evidenced to motivate and demotivate individuals in relation to their performance. If individuals can consciously identify this distinction, then they can re-educate themselves to use those words and phrases which empower them.

A fairly common example would be the exhortation, to ourselves or others, to try harder. Most people respond to the instruction to try harder by becoming more tense and feeling the pressure of the likelihood of not doing well enough. In that state most of us do not give our best because we are not physically or mentally comfortable enough to be able to. If we change that to 'Have another go', we usually elicit a less tense response. It does not have the same judgemental implication and may allow us to treat the next attempt as a chance to improve on the first one.

Of course, the use of language patterns in communicating with others also affects their response. By using words and phrases to which they relate positively, we can elicit more positive responses. We all prefer the doctor who can explain what's wrong with us in simple, everyday terms, to the one who uses technical terms that tell us nothing and make us feel ignorant.

Ecology

Similar techniques to NLP can and have been used in ways that are detrimental to the individual, to others and to the general community. The same basic 'tricks' can be applied to manipulate and disempower others, although they are usually spotted quite quickly because we can distinguish between skilful manipulation and excellence.

In the study of excellence a common thread of ecological awareness and balance was identified as the distinguishing factor. This notion of ecology is based on systems theory which states that any change in one part of the system has a knock-on effect throughout the system. The 'system' may be ourselves, our relationships or our community.

Every genuine NLP technique has a built-in ecology check, to ensure that its use will have a beneficial effect on the person concerned, any others involved and the community at large. Sometimes this is inherent in the way the technique is expressed and presented, i.e. through the language; and sometimes it is a physiological check – the person concerned 'tries on' the effect of the results to check whether he or she will feel comfortable with that effect. This is explicitly using our natural intuitive wisdom rather than just our rational thinking, to ensure that the effect will be beneficial.

We all know this wisdom through wisdom with hindsight – our ability after taking action to know that we knew it wasn't going to work the way we wanted it to. In NLP we use this wisdom as part of the planning and therefore apply it beforehand, when it can usefully help us to adjust our action if necessary.

NLP makes a point of checking ecology beforehand, because most of us would prefer to be acting beneficially if possible. Certainly anyone who wishes to be excellent in what they do wants recognition of their excellence in some way. And we don't recognize as excellent any behaviour which is manipulative or harmful. Ecology checks also will help us to feel safe in experimenting with doing things differently. If I know intuitively that the action will not do any harm, to me or others, then I am more willing to see what happens when I do it.

Outcomes

This element is not unique to NLP. It is generally accepted that we need to think of the results we want before we can plan or take action. However, NLP has developed this theme further. First it is seen as an essential first step to imagine in as much detail as possible the desired state or result. It is not enough to think of a vague statement, such as 'to be happy'. That statement needs to be turned into imagined scenes of what happiness would be: what a person would see, hear and feel if they were happy, how they would be, physically, and what would be going on in their mind.

As this detail is filled in, the ecology checks come into play. The individual can then check if it feels 'right' for them, or if they need to make an adjustment. Then they can imagine how others will react and if that is the reaction they want, and adjust if necessary. Finally they imagine the longer-term effect, on themselves and others. Thus the outcome becomes a fuller, more meaningful description of what they really want. It is a description of the result, the effect on themselves and the effect on others, short term and long term. This gives a perspective which allows the individual to make a more informed choice in their subsequent action.

Moving towards being happy, as an example, may involve someone doing more things to please themselves and therefore fulfilling fewer 'obligations' for their family. They may identify that the initial family reaction to this is quite negative, but longer term the family will come to accept this, and appreciate the enhanced positive state it produces in that person. He or she can then choose whether to deal with the initial reaction, knowing that in the longer term it will pay off, or whether to slow the pace of change of behaviour to reduce that initial reaction. And the person will make this choice by checking which makes them feel more comfortable.

Besides ensuring that the use of the technique will lead to the effect that is really wanted, this detailed spelling-out of the outcome has another benefit. By imagining in such detail the desired outcome the individual makes it more 'real' for themselves. This enables the unconscious to start working on how to achieve the outcome automatically. It's like the difference between thinking a holiday would be a good idea, and collecting holiday brochures and beginning to browse through them. Once we begin to browse we become much clearer about what we really want and also start considering the practical steps we need to take. We will do things like ask others about their experience in certain places or with certain travel companies, notice currency exchange rates and identify clothing we may need to buy to take with us. Our mind now has a filter for noticing things which may help us to put our plans into action effectively and automatically collects those things.

Flexibility

I have already mentioned the importance of flexibility in achieving excellence. It is one of the operating principles of NLP. Flexibility is taken further throughout the practical techniques. Because it is seen as a prerequisite for excellence the NLP techniques include as part of the process the development of choice.

There is an emphasis on developing alternative strategies for achieving an outcome, so that the individual can choose appropriately for the situation rather than have one 'right way' of getting there. This reinforces in practice the idea of feedback rather than failure. If your one 'right way' doesn't work, you've failed; if you have a choice of strategies and one doesn't work, you have feedback to prompt you to try a different strategy.

There are areas of our lives where the idea of choices is built in. For example, if I thought I could do my washing only when there was enough sunshine and warmth to dry it outside, I would spend much of the year accumulating impossible piles of washing. Yet in some activities we can limit ourselves significantly because we have not developed alternative strategies.

Multiple descriptions

This element of NLP links closely to the previous one of flexibility. Part of our flexibility is to be able to consider things from different perspectives and thereby develop multiple descriptions.

Native American Indian culture recognized the value of this in the decision-making activity known as the medicine wheel. In this, those taking part would stand in a circle and each give their own perspective on the issue, thus creating a collective wisdom. No one opinion or view would be taken as 'the true one', and all would be accepted as valid. Similarly, those who are excellent are able to take a variety of perspectives on any issue and thereby enhance and inform their choice.

In NLP people are encouraged to find ways of developing multiple descriptions of issues, strategies, actions and even outcomes.

Besides extending choices, this element also increases appreciation of the differing ways in which people interpret things. We begin to realize that what is the right action in one context or to one person may be the wrong action in another context or to another person. For example, giving advice may help one person but may actually hinder someone else. This leads us towards a lessening of our assumptions and judgements about what is right and wrong, true and false. We become more likely to show respect for other people's views and more careful in finding out what is appropriate and useful in this particular context.

Feedback

The use of feedback to monitor progress is well established. In the study of excellence, NLP has discovered that the level and depth of its use is significantly greater.

Using NLP techniques requires constant monitoring of feedback, verbal and particularly non-verbal, to continue to fine-tune actions and reactions. This brings to a conscious level the unconscious awareness of the slight changes in our physiological and mental reactions which occur constantly, both in ourselves and in those with whom we are interacting. We can then make small adjustments to realign ourselves with the outcome we want, instead of letting it run to the point where it is difficult to change tack. It is like the skilful sailor who constantly makes slight adjustments to keep the boat on course rather than the one who suddenly realizes that they are now eight miles off course and has to significantly change the direction they are heading in, and maybe cope with unexpected currents and dangers as well.

Rapport

Finally, a common thread throughout NLP techniques is the theme of rapport.

In NLP rapport means the formation and maintenance of respectful relationships, and is extended to apply to your relationship with yourself as well as with others. Every NLP technique is dependent for effectiveness on a foundation of rapport, so ways of establishing and maintaining that rapport are implicitly and explicitly built in.

How rapport affects our ability to be at our optimum is exemplified in a description of swimming. If I arrive at the swimming pool out of tune with myself, my swimming is erratic and hard work. As I gain rapport with myself my swimming becomes more flowing. Yet I also need to be aware of others in the pool, because otherwise my performance and theirs will be spoilt through collision or disturbance.

These common threads which appear as elements of all NLP techniques are not something alien to us. They are the explicit statement of what we take into account when we are on form, albeit at an unconscious level. By making them explicit and conscious, NLP gives us the opportunity to identify what we may need to add into our conscious consideration if we want to use our own ability to be excellent more often.

The distinguishing features of NLP

Having considered in some detail the values and common elements of NLP, it is useful to summarize how the NLP approach differs from other approaches to development.

Values and beliefs

The explicit operating principles of NLP set the tone for the whole approach. Throughout the use of NLP there is an explicit attention paid to the beliefs and values which drive our behaviour, and to how we can ensure that the beliefs and values which we hold are useful and respectful to us and to others.

The common elements of NLP

The elements of NLP provide an holistic basis for the approach. Although other approaches to personal development have certainly captured some aspects of how we can become excellent, it is the combination of the totality of the elements which distinguishes NLP techniques.

Universality of application

The whole approach assumes that, for people to be at their optimum, they need only the keys which will allow them to choose their own best practice when they want to. The keys identified in NLP are taken directly from study of human behaviour at its best and have been checked for universality across cultures, gender, age, etc.

Empirical evidence

NLP is firmly based in the empirical reality of human experience. It therefore recognizes the inconsistency and variety of human behaviour and works with that, rather than trying to impose an ideal.

Dealing with the whole person

The approach pays attention to both our intellectual and our physical representation of our experience, and makes us aware of the power of fully integrating the mind, body and heart in our communication.

The methodology used is directed at both the conscious rationality of the person and at their unconscious wisdom. This means that any strategies that person develops are likely to be of benefit to others as well as themselves.

NLP and training and development

As an approach to training and development NLP has some particular features which differ from normal practices.

Strategies for success

The emphasis is on how to achieve optimum performance rather than how to recognize and deal with problems. NLP identifies strategies for success rather than strategies to overcome failure.

Tailor-made excellence

There is no 'best practice'. Instead NLP offers the framework for someone to customize and develop their own 'tailor-made' excellence.

This means that each individual has total ownership of whatever strategies he or she creates and is therefore much more likely to put them into practice. What is more, the approach is non-threatening. It uncovers the natural and recognizable personal resources and wisdom of the individual.

The emphasis is on reminding people of their own best versions, rather than trying to teach them something new and alien, and results in direct empowerment.

The approach also ensures that the responsibility for making a difference is firmly where it belongs – with the individual.

Relevance

The work is very pragmatic and always directly relevant. Clients use their own issues as the focus in any topic area, whether the work is on an individual basis or within a workshop.

Further, the specific issues or situations explored by an individual are his or her own business. The approach is primarily applied in a content-free way – it is not 'what' that is explored, but 'how' and 'how else might it be'. The threat that can be inherent in disclosure is removed.

Effect on performance

The approach deals with the fundamental attitudes and behaviours which underlie excellence and therefore has a generalized effect on performance.

Although the topic for development in which you are using NLP is specific, for example study skills, the same techniques for developing personal excellence can be transferred to a whole variety of situations and contexts.

For the trainer, then, NLP can be an invaluable part of the toolkit, enhancing the effectiveness of the training you offer. The more specific ways in which NLP can be used to make a difference to our training excellence will be discussed in the following chapters.

Part II

The Trainer

In Part I we discussed the context in which trainers are working in order to remind ourselves of the key areas we need to be aware of when examining in more detail our own role in that changing world. I also explained the basic tenets of NLP and how they might help us to develop our skills as trainers.

In the first chapter of this part we will consider in detail how the role of the trainer has changed and is changing, spelling out the key changes which affect us as trainers and the implications for our role in those changes.

In the second chapter, we will examine the personal qualities of the trainer which best support us in our new role. This is an aspect of being a trainer which is not usually considered as an area for discussion or development. Yet, more and more, personal qualities are being taken into account when people apply for jobs. The assumption up to now has been that we have whatever personal qualities we have and if they don't fit, then there is nothing we can do about it. With NLP we can develop the relevant personal qualities to enhance our effectiveness, and I will consider some of the ways we can achieve this.

In the last chapter of this part I will discuss the skills of an excellent trainer and how NLP techniques can enable you to enhance your skills. We will look at those skills which enable us to facilitate learning, the way we train.

No one reading this book will be starting from scratch in any of these areas. You will be aware of the changes in your role, and some of you may be already fulfilling a very different function from when you first began training. You will also have many of the requisite personal qualities – you would not still be in the field of training if you did not have these qualities. And you will already be using facilitating skills to help your learners to succeed. This part is intended to help you identify the areas where you could enhance your excellence further and to suggest ways in which you might do so.

4 The Changing Role of the Trainer

In examining the changing world of organizations and therefore of training, it becomes clear that the trainer's role has shifted dramatically.

In the past the trainer was the expert in a subject area who trained others to improve their skills in that area. A trainer's task was to give information in a logical and coherent way. Training for trainers reflected this bias with its emphasis on the design and delivery of programmes of training.

At the same time there has always been another form of training which was frequently not labelled as such. It is the on-the-job training given by more experienced people to those starting the work. Disparagingly referred to by professional trainers as 'sitting next to Nellie', this informal training was none the less often more effective in making a difference to performance than the formal training event.

Informal trainers did not suffer from the need to prove that they were experts. If they did not know the answer to a question, that question could be used to encourage them to think about possible answers or even to work with the questioner and use them to help to find a solution.

Professional trainers did, however, feel obliged to be experts, and that frequently meant that there was a mimicry of the educational world, where academic and theoretical information was given as much weight (if not more) as practical application. We have all suffered the feeling that we were being blinded by science in a training event, and probably have been caught in the trap as trainers of doing it ourselves to others. Despite the fact that this type of training has never proved to be effective in helping people to learn, many of us have perpetuated its use in order to gain credibility within our professional field.

Fortunately there has been a gradual shift of perspective on the role of the trainer. Among other things, the introduction of participative and experiential methods of training, and more emphasis on the practical results of

47

training, have helped to reduce the degree to which training is seen as an abstract subject. Yet the professional trainer still tends to be seen as an expert in a subject area rather than a training expert.

From expert to enabler of learning and development

What is required in the changing world of training is a fundamental shift in the definition of 'the trainer'. Although some of the required change has come about because trainers themselves want to be more effective, there is still some residual belief about what a trainer should be and do which needs to be removed.

Anyone who has been successful at training is already implicitly making this shift in what they are doing. It is the shift from subject expert to enabler of learning. We cannot be successful in training in the future unless we make this shift and ensure that learning happens rather than training is done.

The changes in practice which have been made are generally not consciously acknowledged and built on. I still come across trainers who apologize for not being theoretical enough, rather than being proud of the fact that they have already moved to a more useful definition of their role.

Recognition of the need for redefinition is now written into the theory of training: we talk about learning theories and learning outcomes, for example. Yet much of the practice is still based on the assumption of expertise in a subject rather than a process of enabling learning. When someone asks 'What do you do?' and you say you're a trainer, they automatically ask 'What in?' – and we answer!

What's more, the process for becoming a trainer still tends to be that we become an expert in a particular area and then add training skills to that, rather than the other way round.

The redefinition of the central role of the trainer as enabler of learning and development brings with it some requirements for further changes in current approaches to training.

Training trainers

The pre-requisites for being a professional trainer become such things as the ability to communicate well and high-level facilitation skills, rather than knowledge of a subject.

The theoretical part of the training needs to emphasize awareness and appreciation of the process of learning and the different ways people learn. This can then be supported by training in a wide repertoire of techniques and approaches for enabling learning, explicitly recognizing the importance of coaching, mentoring, supporting self-directed learning, etc. as part of the trainer's role.

Although there is no doubt that trainer training has moved considerably in this direction, it can still be further improved.

Training functions

For organizational training departments the implications of explicitly defining training as enabling learning and development are far reaching.

First, this would shift training from the periphery to the centre in any organization which is moving towards continuous improvement. If learning is central to the organization's success, then the enablers of learning have a crucial role to play, strategically and practically.

Training has suffered badly from becoming marginalized, often treated as a function which can be out-sourced in organizations which are slimming down and at best being subject to cuts in staff and budget. This redefinition of its function, if carried through in practice, brings it right into the centre of any business.

Second, redefinition of the role of the trainer would, paradoxically, create the specialist role which training has been wanting to achieve. The search for a way to enhance the professional status of trainers has led largely to the expert syndrome. Yet if we become experts in enabling learning we have a useful and effective way of being professional.

Third, the redefinition would require a more integrated function where our work was considered in conjunction with the business development and seen as part of the package, rather than our job being primarily the provision of set programmes.

Marketing and training

Linked to the above point is the change required in the marketing of training. From the perspective of enabling learning and development, training becomes:

- the provision of core learning skills, to enable employees to be effective learners;
- the provision of programmes which encompass a range of learning approaches on and off the job, in areas which are considered to be useful to the development of the business – a responsive provision;
- the identification of opportunities for further development to enable the business to continue to thrive – a pro-active provision;
- the support and reinforcement of managers as primary enablers of learning and development with their staff.

Design of training

Training design needs to become far more contextualized and customized to achieve the specific effects required in the work situation. There would be no such thing as an off-the-shelf course, as these are not designed to be customized. Instead, there would be a package of possible training approaches to a subject, with a repertoire of activities and themes, out of which a customized training solution could be created.

Delivery of training

The trainer in the changing world of training will no longer be limited by the content of a training programme. He or she may be facilitating, coaching one-to-one, presenting, running workshops, training others to train or introducing self-managed learning. This would give scope for creative permutations of training approaches and make some very different demands from traditional training. The method(s) of delivery would be decided on by considering the required effect in the workplace and the most appropriate methods of enabling learning for that effect.

No doubt all experienced trainers have already moved some way towards this different approach to training, for two primary reasons:

1. The satisfaction in training is having evidence that you have enabled learning, and so we tend towards those approaches which will give us this result.
2. To have some influence in the changing world of organizations we have to have begun to cater for their differing requirements from training.

It is still necessary to move further into the role of enabler of learning. This role is not generally acknowledged or recognized, and there is a long history of training being an 'added extra' which is undertaken when there is the time and budget for it. As trainers, we have to create a different view of what we can offer to the organization, and be proactive in promoting the vital role we can play in a learning organization.

The trainer as facilitator

The first clear difference in our role of trainer needs to be its redefinition as 'enabling learning and development'. We will be facilitators of the process of learning in all situations.

A facilitator is defined as someone who makes things easy for others. In training this has tended to be interpreted as applying only to a particular approach to encouraging development. For example, we may facilitate the process of developing a team vision by helping the team to structure their thinking and approach to the task.

With the changing role of the trainer, this process of facilitation will apply throughout the function of training. It begins with the identification of learning opportunities, looking for ways to make learning and development attractive, useful and viable for people.

We need to market those opportunities in a way which makes it easy for people to make an informed choice, and to offer a range of ways of achieving the learning, so as to allow for the variety of ways in which people learn most effectively.

The last two aspects of facilitation are even more demanding of us. The first requirement is to make it easy to evaluate what we are offering in terms of making a difference in the workplace. The implication is that we open up the possibility of more direct and inescapable criticism of how we are fulfilling our role by giving people tangible results to expect as a result of the particular development programme – no more hiding behind the intangible 'soft' possible results! This requires us to let go of our mystique of expertise and be more vulnerable to the feedback of our customers.

The second requirement is to facilitate the skills of supporting learning and development in others. When we are working with managers, they will need not only to develop their own skills but also to know how to develop the skills of those who work with them. We are therefore training the line managers to train.

This again requires letting go of the mystique of expertise which suggests that only professional trainers can enable the learning of others, and finding ways of dealing with the vulnerability of letting go our traditional role: the more managers are able to train others, the less the professional trainer will be required to do so.

Despite these apparent anomalies in being a facilitator, taking on this function creates of itself a different and perhaps more important role for the trainer. We become the educators and supporters of a learning organization – crucial elements of a changing organization.

As both internal and external pressures to change our approach increase, many trainers will feel that they are in unknown territory where they are less confident of their ability to deliver effectively.

What is more, there are important aspects of the changing role which, as it were, put us in the spotlight as we venture into this unknown territory, so we can't even practise in secret before exposing ourselves to the scrutiny of those who are expecting us to fulfil our role differently.

However, most of us are in the business of training because we are interested in learning, and our own process of development is of itself useful in the changing role we are adopting. We can utilize our own development to help others to undertake their development to be successful in the changing world.

The trainer as a model of good practice

If we are to become the educators and supporters of a learning organization then we must recognize the fact that people learn most from how others are rather than what they talk about.

This involves a significant change in people's attitude and approach to learning and development, and this type of shift is achieved only when there are clear examples to show that:

- it is effective in achieving the results wanted;
- it works for the benefit of the individual as well as the organization.

When the East Europeans had young girls as their gymnastic representatives in the Olympics, and they were medal winners, the model of training very young children specifically for this purpose looked attractive: it was obviously effective in achieving the results required. However, the limitations that such stringent training put on the lives of those representatives became clear, and the model became less attractive: there was not enough benefit for the individual.

By contrast, there are now models in the field of world-class athletics which clearly offer a more rounded picture. The athlete appears as dedicated to his or her chosen sport and also as a rounded personality, someone with other interests and abilities. Through what they do and how they are they seem to model the possibility of world-class achievement in the field linked to the development of other aspects of personal potential – a much more attractive model.

So as trainers we can be important models of the benefits of making fundamental changes, both to the organization and to the individual.

The trainer as a model of learning

The first aspect of the changes which we can model is the change from expert to learner. Setting an example by being a learner is actually made easier by the change in our own role. We are learning how to do things differently, and by acknowledging that fact we make it easier for others to do the same about their roles.

If we can also demonstrate that we are gaining from being a learner, rather than being uncomfortable in that position, we encourage others to begin to redefine what being a learner means.

There has been a tendency for learning to be seen as the difficult stage one has to go through in order to achieve the result of being recognized as knowledgeable. It has not been seen as a desirable state in itself, but rather as a necessary evil. Consequently, people are reluctant to admit that they don't know the answer, because that represents a loss of face. Education and training have reinforced this attitude by promoting their wares as being more and more sophisticated sets of answers rather than more and more encouragement to be a learner.

Yet those of us who have rediscovered the love of learning, which came naturally to us as small children, know that continuous learning as a way of life brings with it enormous personal benefits.

Life is far more interesting when you are constantly looking for opportunities to increase your awareness and develop your skills. It is also less stressful to admit that you don't know, or that you got it wrong, and then to put your energy into finding out or experimenting with different approaches, than it is to try and cover up and pretend that you do know. By explicitly admitting that we don't always know the best way, and by welcoming feedback and using it to improve and refine our repertoire of possibilities, we can set an example of continuous learning that encourages others to do the same.

Modelling flexibility

As a trainer experimenting with different approaches to enabling learning we can model the flexibility which is essential in a changing world. By letting go our old assumptions of what training is and being prepared to try new approaches to facilitate learning we are setting an example of flexibility which others can follow in their own roles.

Modelling continuous improvement

The above aspects of setting an example combine to help us to offer a model of continuous improvement. This is still a relatively new concept for most people, and although it may be appealing the question remains of how to do it.

By being someone who proactively seeks to extend their repertoire of skills, strategies and knowledge, we are demonstrating how to improve continuously, on a day-to-day basis. This also gives us a future orientation. Questions like 'If this was good enough today, how could it be even better tomorrow?' or 'What else might enable you to perform even more effectively in the future?' become part of our everyday vocabulary.

Modelling fun

Last but not least, we need to model the personal benefits of being a continuous learner. When we actively adopt this approach it produces an enthusiasm, curiosity and sense of fun in learning which resembles our initial approach to learning as small children.

It is the fact that learning is enjoyable and livens up our life that is most appealing to others, at an unconscious level. We need to challenge the belief that learning is hard work and painful which so many carry with them from previous experience of formal learning situations.

The trainer of the future, then, will be a very different animal from the stereo-typical trainer of the past. In order to fulfil this changing role, we will need to call on some different aspects of our personal qualities and professional skills. NLP is specifically intended to enable us to call on our own excellence to help us to extend beyond our present limitations.

So we will begin by considering how NLP can help to extend our qualities and skills.

5 The Qualities of the Excellent Trainer

In this chapter we will be examining the personal qualities which we can develop to enable us to be excellent trainers. In the past our personal qualities have not been the first consideration when we looked at our development needs. We were more likely to start with clearly job-related skills, such as presentation. Now, just as is happening for other employees, we need to start with our personal development. To work in a changing environment everyone requires the flexibility and willingness to change that will equip them for an uncertain future. We are an important model of that requirement, and if we are to promote it with others convincingly we must start with ourselves.

Personal beliefs and values

The first area to examine is that of our personal beliefs and values. Although often an unconscious part of our make-up, these have a significant effect on our behaviour and attitudes and can often sabotage our conscious intentions. It is therefore worth finding ways of aligning our beliefs and values with what we want to achieve. We have four sets of beliefs and values: those we have about ourselves; those we have about other people; those we have about information and those we have about 'how the world works'.

Beliefs and values concerning ourselves

When we think about or talk about ourselves we reveal our beliefs and values concerning ourselves. We have some sort of mental checklist of what we can or can't do or be.

How do we formulate this checklist?

We begin by collecting things others say to us when we're children, and this has often set a negative tone to the assessment of ourselves. It is more likely that adults remarked on what we weren't good at, than what we were good at. A parent may have told us we were clumsy, a teacher may have told us that we were lacking concentration. Their intention was not usually harmful but the results can be devastating for our self-esteem. Having first heard the statement of how others see us, we begin to unconsciously collect evidence that confirms that view. And, of course, the more you believe that you are clumsy, the more likely you are to be clumsy and give yourself yet more evidence that it's true!

However, once we realize that this list of beliefs about ourselves is based on what is really an arbitrary collection of evidence, sparked off by things said to us in childhood, we can begin to revise our checklist to make it more useful. After all, for every example of your being clumsy there is probably an example of your being skilful – it's just that you weren't collecting that evidence.

So the first stage of improving our excellence as trainers is to review our beliefs about ourselves and ensure that they are aligned to what we want to achieve.

Reviewing your beliefs and values about yourself

As we considered the changing role of the trainer it became clear that the excellent trainer needs personal qualities which will support the expanded role now required of him or her.

Stop and take a little while to produce your own version of the ideal checklist of the qualities of an excellent trainer: what is he or she like, what can he or she do. (You will find an example of such a checklist at the end of this chapter (Appendix 5.1) to compare with your own or to get you started.)

Now go through your list and tick all those qualities which you believe are already a part of you. At this point, it is important that you give yourself credit and recognition for what you know you already have as beliefs in yourself. We often skip through this stage and fail to affirm our basic resources, so make sure that you really give yourself credit for the qualities which you have already developed well.

Now go through the list considering each of the qualities which you have not yet ticked. First, check that you are not being over-modest: most people are accustomed to under-assessing themselves. Recognize that quality if you have it even if it isn't consistent or as strong as you would like it to be.

If that quality still doesn't earn a tick, stop and search through your personal history, consciously looking for examples of where you may have demonstrated it. These examples may come from any sphere of your life: for example, you may have been particularly tolerant with a niece or nephew, rather than a work colleague.

The purpose in finding these examples is to remind yourself that you do have these qualities even if they are not in regular use. Finding an example is the adult equivalent of the child accepting a statement about them from a parent or teacher: it is beginning to notice and create more evidence to support that particular belief.

By the time you have completed this second stage of reviewing the checklist there should be few, if any, of the qualities of an excellent trainer that you feel are not a part of who you are. We will consider later on how we can develop qualities of which we are not yet fully confident.

To begin with, what matters is that you extend your beliefs about what you can be like so that you acknowledge your own potential resources.

So, to complete this review, we need to now embed the useful beliefs about yourself as an excellent trainer in your unconscious. This is a simple task: we begin to accept beliefs when we give them as clear statements to ourselves, expressed as affirmations. An affirmation is expressed in the positive – what I am, not what I am not – and begins with 'I am' or 'I can'. Examples of this might be 'I am tolerant' and 'I can communicate well'.

So, take your checklist of the qualities of an excellent trainer and rewrite it, with 'I can' or 'I am' in front of each quality, to create affirmative statements. Then read all the statements out loud slowly to yourself, and as you read out each one allow yourself to remember an example of your demonstrating that quality.

You have now laid the foundation in your unconscious for the beliefs about yourself which will support you as an excellent trainer. From now on, you will notice when you demonstrate those qualities and will also notice opportunities for developing them.

Beliefs and values concerning others

The set of beliefs and values we hold concerning others is created in our unconscious in the same way as the beliefs and values about ourselves. We 'collect' them, mostly in childhood, and then collect evidence to support them.

Most of us have a wide spectrum of beliefs about others and use 'clues' to decide which ones to apply. For example, we may have particular beliefs about what people are like which are triggered by certain types of accent, or we may apply one set of beliefs about people to friends and another set to work colleagues.

This stereotyping is largely unconscious and is intended to be useful to us. It helps us to choose how we will react and respond to others. However, it is less useful when our stereotype is a negative one as it unconsciously creates in us expectations of how that person will be, and we respond to our expectations more than their actual behaviour.

For example, most teenagers have at some point come home later than they promised. And most expect their parents to be angry. They therefore are either defensive or trying to avoid a confrontation. The anxious parent who has been worrying about their safety quickly turns into the angry parent they were expecting.

As a trainer we need to be aware of how our beliefs about people as learners will affect our expectations and therefore their behaviour as learners.

Reviewing your beliefs and values about others

The process of reviewing this set of beliefs is the same as for reviewing beliefs about yourself.

1. What would be a useful set of beliefs about learners for an excellent trainer? NLP has some explicit beliefs on the theme, which are proven to be useful:

    ● Everyone makes the best choice available to them at the time.
    ● We each already have all the resources we need to be wise and excellent.
    ● We are naturally learning creatures, as exemplified in childhood.

    What other statements can you think of? Create your own ideal checklist. (You will find an example of such a checklist at the end of this chapter (Appendix 5.1) and can use it to compare with your own or to get you started.)
2. Go through your list and tick those beliefs which you already hold.
3. Go through the list again and search through your experience for examples to begin to support some of the statements you haven't yet ticked. Remember to use informal learning experiences as well as formal ones. For example, you may not find any active learners, who ask for help in their own preferred way of learning, in the formal learning situation. But in informal learning there are likely to be several, such as the child wanting to learn how to cook.
4. You may still have some statements about others as learners which you can find no support for, but by now, most items on your list should be evidenced, at least to some degree.
5. We now need to embed these beliefs into your unconscious as your expectations of others as learners.

    Begin with those you already hold, and reaffirm them by writing them down again and saying them out loud, remembering, at the same time, examples of evidence.

    Take the second set, where you eventually thought of examples, and express them as, for example: 'People can decide for themselves the best way for them to learn'. As you write them down, think again of your example.

Take the third set, which is any statements which you couldn't find supporting evidence for, and express them as : 'I want to believe that people...'. As you write them down, imagine how someone would react in a particular learning situation if they were like that.

You have now laid the foundation in your unconscious for the beliefs about others as learners which will support you as an excellent trainer. From now on, you will notice evidence to support these beliefs and opportunities to create such evidence.

Beliefs and values about information

I include this set of beliefs because information is central to training. Formulated in the same way as other beliefs, what we believe about information affects the way we present it.

What most of us hold as beliefs about information have been unconsciously absorbed from what others have told us or indicated about their beliefs. Some commonly held beliefs in Western industrialized culture are:

- Information is a good thing;
- Information is power;
- Information only has value if it's relevant;
- Valuable information is difficult to understand.

To be an excellent trainer, what are the useful values and beliefs about information that you can embed in your unconscious? Write a short paragraph that you feel sums it up and then read it aloud to yourself. To help you to do this, think of a time when you received information which had a positive effect on your life and review what made it valuable. You may begin with 'Information is valuable when...' (You will find an example of such a paragraph at the end of the chapter and can use it to compare with your own or to get you started.)

Next, consider our beliefs about particular information which we need to put across to others. If we have not found a way to make it meaningful for ourselves, then we will not present it in a way which makes it meaningful for others.

An example of this is the often-seen result of customer care training, where people say the 'correct' words, but give them no meaning. 'How can I help?', said in a sulky voice with no eye contact and no smile, does not make the customer feel cared for.

If I, as a trainer, do not believe that the information I am giving will make a difference, then my indifference is the message that my trainees pick up, whether consciously or unconsciously.

We therefore need to consider the specific information we are going to convey and ask ourselves 'How can I make this information meaningful to me?' and 'How can I make this information meaningful for them?'. If the information itself does not seem valuable then we need to find some useful application of it.

Many years ago, when I was a teacher, I was told to instruct my classes that they must obey a new school rule: to stand still in a straight line in silence outside the classroom before entering for the next lesson. This seemed to me perfectly designed for sabotage. As a teacher, I could see long minutes being taken off my lesson time as I tried to enforce this rule. I chose to present it to my classes as an example of a rule which is not particularly useful but also not worth the trouble of breaking. I acknowledged the positive intentions behind the rule: to improve self-discipline, to begin the lesson in an ordered, quiet way, but admitted that I didn't think that of itself it would create these results. However, I helped the students to think through the likely consequences of sabotaging the rule so that they could see that their life would be easier if they obeyed it. I then asked them to consider how we could turn it into a positive rule, and got some interesting responses that we acted on. In this way I was able to make the information useful: the head got the results he wanted, much to his surprise; I felt comfortable because I had made the information valuable; and the students responded well and learned something more about how to turn apparent negatives into positives.

Our beliefs affect our behaviour, and others are aware if our words and our behaviour don't match. It is vital that, as trainers, we are able to find ways of making information meaningful if we are to convince others of its value. They are convinced by how we are as we present it much more than by our just having a superficial formula of presentation.

Beliefs about how the world works

These beliefs are a central part of our core beliefs and are very powerful in affecting how we interpret what happens in our lives. For example, those who believe there's no such thing as coincidence look for and usually find meaning in such 'occurrences'. Those who believe that coincidences are just accidental will take no particular notice of them and may not even notice them at all.

Many of the explicit beliefs in NLP are in this category of 'how the world works'. They imply that we can have control over our destiny and that we do in fact create it by the choices we consciously or unconsciously make.

Trainers are affected, both personally and in the work we do with others, by what we perceive as possible in the world we live in. It's important therefore to consider this category of core beliefs as a part of the package of useful beliefs for excellence. If I believe that you must have at least a degree to succeed in business, then that belief will negatively affect my expectations of non-graduates. Or if I believe that we are mostly governed by circumstances beyond our control, then I will have a very limited view of personal empowerment.

Review of beliefs and values about how the world works

Begin this review by looking through again the NLP presuppositions. They are the beliefs which excellent people hold to be true and use to drive their behaviour and actions. They are proven to elicit excellence in self and in others. Which of these could you use to begin your ideal checklist of useful beliefs for an excellent trainer? Express them in your own words. Now, what other core beliefs about how the world works would be useful? Add them to the list. (You will find an example of such a checklist at the end of the chapter (Appendix 5.1) and can use it to compare with your own or to get you started.)

Next, as before, go through the list, ticking those beliefs you already hold. Go through a second time, consciously looking for any evidence in your experience that would support those beliefs.

Finally, embed these beliefs in your unconscious. Take all those you have some evidence for, and rewrite them as 'I believe that . . .' statements, saying each one out loud and thinking, as you do so of evidence you have. Now write the rest down as 'I want to believe that . . .' statements, and when you say each one out loud add 'and I will begin to look for supporting evidence from now on'.

Dealing with limiting beliefs

In this consideration of beliefs you may have noticed that we have not dealt with negative or limiting beliefs which we may hold. By this I mean the beliefs which hold us back and that we are still convinced are true. They are often expressed as 'Yes, but . . .' statements – for example, 'But people don't change easily, particularly as they get older'.

The normal approach would be to start with these, analyse them and try to argue ourselves logically out of them. However, beliefs are not logical, even if we have created a logic to justify them. Opposite beliefs can be held by two people and both can defend and justify them totally, from their own perspective. As I have already described, beliefs are formed when we take someone else's belief or statement and find evidence to support it from our own experience. They are usually not consciously chosen but, rather, unconsciously accepted because they seem to fit at the time.

The fastest way to deal with our limiting beliefs is to consciously choose to adopt some different ones and actively look for evidence to support the new beliefs – the process of review I have described. As we do this the old beliefs begin to lose their influence over us. This is our natural process for changing beliefs. For example, as children we believe that parents are wise, but as we grow up, we need to find ways of asserting our individuality apart from them, so we begin to look for evidence of their fallibility. After a while we develop a new belief, that parents are just human beings, and the old belief loses its power.

The only differences between the process I have been proposing to you and our natural process are that:

1. you are making conscious choices about what beliefs will be useful to you;
2. the process is speeded up by taking conscious action to make it happen.

If you want to take more action to reduce the power of your limiting beliefs, then you can go through a ritual for letting go of them. First, list them on paper. You can go through the four categories again and note down all the negative or self-limiting beliefs you hold in each category. Now take the paper, and either screw it up and burn it, or tear it up and put it in the bin. As you do so, say to yourself, 'I am letting go of these beliefs. I now have space for more useful beliefs to have a positive influence on my life!'

Using the checklists

We have now established some checklists of the beliefs which are useful for an excellent trainer. These are not final versions, so you may find that you think of additional or different statements which you want to add, as we continue to consider how we enhance our excellence as trainers. Remember that there is no 'perfect' checklist. Each of us will have different emphases in what we consider to be a useful belief, and different priorities. What is more, we will adapt and change those lists as we continue to enhance our excellence.

We can use the full checklists as reminders to ourselves of what we choose to have governing our attitudes and behaviour. We can also select those beliefs we consider to be most important in helping us to be at our best in training, and repeat those few to ourselves as part of our preparation, thereby reinforcing those commands in our unconscious.

Finally, we can choose a few of the beliefs for which we want to collect more evidence and consciously create opportunities to get that evidence so as to strengthen those beliefs.

What we believe governs our expectations, our judgements and our actions, whether we are conscious of it or not. This has been acknowledged in the field of training, but has been seen as an almost impossible area to tackle.

Through studying what excellent people hold as beliefs and how beliefs are changed, NLP can offer strategies which enable us to create for ourselves a powerful set of beliefs as the foundation for developing ourselves at the levels of attitude and behaviour.

Your ideal checklist of useful beliefs for excellence in training provides you with the guiding principles for the other areas of development.

Setting an example

The second area relating to our personal qualities which is worth paying some attention to is related to the model we provide to others – how we set an example.

When we are engaged in paradigm shifts, as is the case in organizations and in training, it is important to have new role models which demonstrate the behaviour and the effects which result from taking on the new paradigm.

First, these role models give us the inspiration or motivation to at least try out something new. For example, it is seeing friends who are obviously benefiting from the freedom inherent in being able to drive that often spurs us on to learn to drive ourselves. Someone else who is obviously benefiting in some way from the change provides us with evidence to support the belief that maybe we can do it too. More importantly, if it seems to benefit the individual we are attracted towards the possibility. We are essentially selfish creatures: if I can't see any personal benefit for me, I am unlikely to want to be involved. Others benefiting gives me clues about how I might also benefit.

We also learn more from models and examples than we do from being taught or trained. We naturally pick up behaviours and attitudes from models or examples in our environment, and because this happens unconsciously we don't feel as if we have had to work hard to make that development. Just think of all the behaviours we learned, as children, from our parents. And remember, in particular, all the less desirable aspects of that learning – where we did what they did rather than what they said we should do! This illustrates perfectly why it is not only important to know that you are a model, but also to be aware of what exactly you are modelling.

So what are we modelling for others?

The important aspects of modelling

Learning

We are able, as trainers, to provide a model for the changing approach to learning.

The first part of that is not just to accept, but to delight in being in a continuous learning process – a learner.

We are learning to tackle our role and function differently, so the label of learner is true for us. What matters is that we exemplify a positive approach to learning: that it's fun; that it's acceptable to experiment and admit that you're not sure if it will work; that it's something to be proud of, not ashamed of; that you may make mistakes and can go back, learn from them, and try again as part of the learning; and that you actively seek out opportunities for learning rather than always playing safe.

What is more, this model has to be in place throughout our working day, not only when we're formally training. So it applies in our informal interactions with people as well.

Continuous development

We should also be demonstrating some of the qualities which we are advocating as essential in a continuous development environment: flexibility of approach, use of initiative and personal empowerment are key phrases for this.

These qualities relate to being a model of learning, and go further. The trainer who can not only agree that he or she needs to try a different approach but also can decide to do so on the spot, and has another idea ready to experiment with, is a far more powerful model than the trainer who agrees that this isn't working and then loses confidence and says that they need to go away and ask permission to try a different approach.

Respect

We must live the statement 'People matter'.

Our manner of relating to others – showing respect, encouraging development, treating them as we wish to be treated, valuing their diversity – will give important messages about the genuineness of the statement and how it is vital to continuous development.

Personal benefit

Finally, this needs to be an attractive model – one which is of obvious benefit to you personally and something which is demonstrably enjoyable, stimulating and rewarding. If you find it stressful to act in this way, then others will pick up your stress signals, however much you try to hide them. It is important to find a way of making the modelling of these qualities easy for you, and we will consider how to do that.

I have spelt out a demanding description of the trainer as role model. If we want to be influential in the changing organization then we will take the steps required to be this model. We influence the attitudes and behaviours of others more by how we are than by what we say, so we need strategies to help us to embody fully the qualities we have listed here.

Developing ourselves as a model change agent

How do we fulfil this model? The first step is to convince yourself that it's worth the effort. What benefits will there be for you, in adopting this role as model?

List all the benefits which occur to you, including positive effects for you personally and positive results in the effect you have on others. (If you want to compare your list with others, there is a sample list of benefits in Appendix 5.2 at the end of this chapter.)

If your list is not yet full enough to be convincing to you, read through the descriptions of the important aspects of modelling and add any of those you think would be beneficial.

Now you can begin the process of developing yourself as a model. To do this simply we can use NLP techniques which enable us to bring together a customized version of our own best practice in these qualities. After all, we have at some point been unconsciously excellent in all these areas. However it may not have been appropriate for the context in which you will now be demonstrating it. For example, you may have demonstrated the qualities of an excellent learner when you were learning amateur photography at evening classes, but your behaviour as a learner when you were quite clearly classified as a learner may not be appropriate for your role as a learner and a trainer.

The NLP approach deals with this problem directly because what you take from previous experience is not the behaviour but the state. What the study of excellence discovered was that people tend to have the same type of physical and mental state whenever they are performing excellently. They have an excellent listening state, alert state, learning state, etc. If they adopt this physical and mental state they will automatically adapt their behaviour to fit the context. What is more, each individual has a unique way of 'setting themselves up', physically and mentally, for excellence. So an excellent listening state for one person will be slightly different from the excellent listening state of another person. Consequently you cannot describe the 'perfect' listening state and teach people that version, because their own will be a unique adaptation that fits them perfectly as opposed to the off-the-peg version which isn't so perfectly suited to them. This makes the NLP approach far more powerful in helping individuals to be at their best than the usual 'here's what you have to do' guidelines that are offered in most behavioural development texts and courses.

It follows that if you can identify some key features of your own physical and mental state when you have demonstrated the qualities you wish to model, you can then consciously 'set yourself up' to be in that excellent state again and make it far easier for yourself to be the model you want to be.

The way in which we find out about our own ideal states follows the process we already use, unconsciously, to elicit different states in ourselves.

In any given situation we unconsciously absorb information about how we are, physically, mentally and emotionally. In other words, we describe to ourselves our present state. Having gathered that information, we then unconsciously attach to it a trigger – something to remind us of that state again. This may be a sound, or phrase, something we can see, or a symbol, or just a physical movement or gesture. From then on, whenever that trigger reappears we will automatically resume that state unless we consciously decide to counteract it.

This sounds very complex, but it is actually very simple. Think of a partic-ular piece of music you like. If you take note, you will find that it always puts you in the same mood, even if you hear a snatch of it by chance. This mood is a particular physical, mental and emotional state and the music is the trigger for you. Now think of a photograph or picture that you like. The same thing happens. Every time you look at it it puts you in a particular mood – another trigger.

This is what happens naturally, so that we don't consciously set up our state most of the time – we are triggered into it by some stimulus and then act from that state. I have given you two positive examples, but there are many less useful states which we unconsciously adopt in response to triggers. These do not elicit our best – anything but! No doubt you can think of several such examples.

By spelling out consciously our natural unconscious process for creating our state, NLP gives us the opportunity to take some conscious control of this process:

1. by creating particularly useful states for ourselves;
2. by knowing how to switch on the state we want rather than cope with the state we've got.

So, to revert to how to create your own state of excellence as a model, here is the process by which you can do so.

Process for creating an excellent state

1. Define the state you want to be able to re-create. Use the section on what we are modelling to select the quality you want to demonstrate and express that quality in your own words, for example: 'clearly valuing others' different viewpoints'.
2. Remember a time when you did demonstrate this quality. It doesn't matter what the context was, or how long you were like this. Accept any example your mind comes up with, even if you're not sure it's the best one. Our minds are very good at finding appropriate examples for this activity, even if they are not ones we would deliberately select.
3. Now allow yourself to go back into that moment of excellence. Remember the setting, the others involved, and relive the moment.
4. As you go back into the moment fully, begin to notice information about yourself in that state – and if you're not sure you can remember the information accurately, imagine what it would be. First, notice anything you can see there which draws your attention – or that you don't notice anything in particular.
5. Notice anything you can hear in that situation, sounds in the environment – or that you don't hear anything much.
6. How does it feel to be demonstrating this quality well? Notice where you feel the satisfaction, what sensations you have.
7. Pay more attention to your actual physical state. Are you mobile or still? Which muscles in your limbs, your torso, your shoulders, are tense and which relaxed? Notice what makes you physically comfortable when demonstrating this quality, and if there is any particular posture or gesture associated with it.
8. Examine your facial expression, how it changes and stays the same as you demonstrate this quality. Notice if your jaw is clenched, what your eyes are like, and if your head is on one side or straight on your body. Notice how you speak – tone and speed and loudness.
9. Now go inside yourself and notice how you are breathing – fast or slow, deeply or shallowly.
10. What goes on inside your head when you're demonstrating this quality? Do you picture anything in your imagination or is the internal video screen empty? Do you say anything to yourself, or is the internal tape recorder silent? This is the type of information which you unconsciously collect in any situation. You then need to process it.

11. Staying in that situation where you are demonstrating the quality you want to re-create, allow all the information you have collected to filter down through your consciousness, and then ask yourself:

   ● What could I picture to myself that would instantly remind me of this state?
   ● What could I say to myself that would instantly remind me of this state?

   Allow answers to spring to mind, and don't judge them – they may or may not be the logical conscious choice you would make. Triggers are frequently illogical, and we are creating triggers here.

12. Come back to the present and confirm to yourself these two triggers, which will enable you to re-create the whole state, by saying to yourself: 'From now on, whenever I picture x, or say y to myself, I will automatically regain the physical, mental and emotional state I have when demonstrating my (quality) excellently.' You may like to record your triggers, to reinforce the reminder.

This process can now be repeated with each of the qualities you wish to develop further, so that you have a set of triggers for creating the appropriate state.

If you want to combine them into a state called 'the model change agent', then you can take a final step in the process. This requires consideration of all the states and triggers you have now collected. Look through your record and say to yourself: 'I now want to combine all these states to produce the state of an excellent change agent.' As I imagine myself integrating these states into one, and stepping into the state of excellent change agent, I can ask:

● What will I picture to evoke this integrated state?
● What will I say to myself to evoke this integrated state?

And you now will have two triggers to create that integrated physical and mental state which will help you to demonstrate this set of qualities well. In order to go through this process more easily you may find it useful to tape-record the steps, leaving a short space between each instruction.

The triggers you have chosen for yourself are very powerful in setting you up to demonstrate the qualities in a way which suits you and your personality. You need to consciously choose to use them. In any situation, just take a breath-space before you begin and imagine one or both of your triggers. You will now have the right 'mood' from which to act and react appropriately.

Using models of excellence

You may feel that some of the qualities required of an excellent trainer are ones which you want to demonstrate even better than you have done in the past. When we feel this way it usually means that we have noticed others who seem to have an even better version of that quality and we are unconsciously comparing ourselves with them.

The fastest way to develop our own qualities further is to use in a conscious way those people we consider excellent as models to help us. For example, when I came across a trainer who could handle an audience of 150 as if they were a small group I realized that I could learn from him about establishing relationships and improve on my relating qualities.

Using a model of excellence consciously requires that we collect a different quality of information about that person. It's not what they do but how they are that gives us the useful information. The same things we notice about ourselves in an excellent state are the things to notice about a model of excellence: what they are like, physically; how they breathe; how they speak. If we can question the person we should ask what they are paying attention to in the environment around them, visually and aurally; what they are picturing and/or saying to themselves; what sensations they have.

Once we have as much information as we can get we then need to 'try it on', as a way of being. Most importantly, we now need to adjust it to suit us as individuals. This fine-tuning is the vital step which makes a model useful. In my example, I realized that he caught the eye of every individual in the audience. I was comfortable with that, when I tried it. He also was very mobile physically. I found I needed to be still when establishing that contact, because being mobile was not comfortable and distracted me.

When we use models unconsciously we naturally make these adjustments to make the model fit us individually. I may be like my mother in some ways, but I'm like her in my own way. If the person seems to have a very different personality from ours we will not use that person as a model because of the degree of adjustment required to make the model fit. However, when we're using a model of excellence consciously we can select those elements of the information we have acquired which do fit or which are easily adjusted. We are not copying the person, we are using some of their characteristics as a pattern to help us to develop ourselves.

Monitoring and reviewing the development of our personal qualities

What I have proposed so far is how to lay the foundation for developing further our personal qualities. To build consciously on that foundation we can instigate a simple monitoring and review process for ourselves.

First, we can get into the habit of noticing times when we are demonstrating the qualities which make a difference. Each day, simply recall any times when you were being an excellent learner, or flexible in approach, or demonstrating some other quality. This takes only moments but is very powerful in building up our unconscious patterns for continuing to act in ways which demonstrate these qualities.

Second, we can begin to use the times when we revert to old habits to rehearse being different. Each day, select one situation where you were not demonstrating the qualities you aim for. Now imagine how it would have been different if you had demonstrated the qualities of an excellent trainer. Play through the revised version in your head, maybe a couple of times. Again, this doesn't take long but is a powerful way of improving our performance.

This whole process follows the natural pattern of what we do anyway, unconsciously, to reinforce our behaviour. Most of us sit and review our day in some way, but what we tend to do is to concentrate on what went wrong or didn't go as well as we would have liked. In fact we can replay totally disastrous moments over and over again. What this does is to reinforce the unconscious pattern for doing exactly the same thing again – and most of us have experienced this. For example, there may be someone you work with who seems to bring out the worst in you and you end up arguing with each other. You replay the scene in your head and declare that you won't let it happen again. But you haven't 'rehearsed' an alternative – so it does happen again!

By consciously using our natural ability to reinforce our unconscious patterns we can make this ability to live a scene in our imagination into a positive asset, reinforcing positive traits and improving on less developed ones. As we continue to review our practice, consciously noticing examples of when we demonstrate the qualities of an excellent trainer and rehearsing improved versions of our not-so-good moments, we begin to build up the patterns which enable us to be more and more unconsciously excellent in these respects. We also begin to develop a body of evidence about the useful effects of demonstrating these qualities so that we become increasingly motivated to use them. They are, after all, the personal qualities which help to create excellence, and are positives in their own right.

Appendix 5.1

The Excellent Trainer

Beliefs about self

Is a learner
Is flexible
Is tolerant of other viewpoints
Is curious
Is non-judgemental
Is willing to take risks
Is innovative
Is enthusiastic
Is helpful
Encourages feedback
Can communicate on different levels
Can guide others constructively in developments
Can explain in ways which others can understand
Can acknowledge their own errors or lack of knowledge
Is interested in what others do
Can identify where people are starting from
Can identify outcomes and effects of development
Finds learning fun
Uses initiative
Is empowered
Shows respect for others
Looks for the positives

Checks rather than assumes
Influences with integrity
Likes people
Gives recognition
Has a repertoire of alternative strategies
Can recognize the needs of individuals
Can always see opportunities for developing themselves further
Is willing to try something different if what they're doing isn't working
Takes responsibility for getting their message across

Beliefs about learners

Everyone makes the best choice available to them at the time
We already have all the resources we need to be wise and excellent
We are naturally learning creatures
People want to develop their potential
People are willing to learn if learning is offered in the right way for them
People learn by example rather than by teaching
People need to practise, not just learn to discuss
People learn more when it's fun
People are learning all the time
People will take risks if they are made to feel safe in doing so
People doing something always have ideas about how to do it better
People know more than they think they know
People can decide for themselves the best way for them to learn
Everyone has some special gift(s)
We all need to find some personal benefit to motivate us to learn

Beliefs about information

Information is valuable when it results in some form of development. In order to be valuable it needs to be useful and relevant. When giving information to others we need to ensure that it is expressed in language they understand and that it is related to their situation or context. Information to be used for development needs to be translated into action and/or results. Any information given needs to be followed by the question 'So what difference will it make to you?' or 'How can you use this information to make a difference?'

Beliefs about how the world works

All behaviour is communication
Every failure is an opportunity for development
We create the story of our lives
We are a mind, body and spirit combined, and work best when all are working together
The journey to excellence never ends
The world is a place of abundance
When we are attuned to ourselves and the world around us, magic happens
It is individuals who change the world
Everyone wants the best that is possible
Integrity brings its own reward
We always have a choice
We are creators, not victims
Anything we can imagine is possible

Appendix 5.2

The Benefits of Being a Change Agent Model

I will enjoy the challenge
I will be preparing myself for a changing world
I will learn a lot
It gives me permission to experiment and try out new things
It will make my job more interesting
It will make my job more rewarding
I will develop a wider repertoire of ways of responding
I will enhance my relationship with others
I will feel that I am in the forefront of development
I will be able to encourage others
I will enhance my value to the organization
It will be easier to convince others that change is worthwhile
It will be easier to work with others if I don't always have to get it right
It will give me a renewed sense of purpose
I will feel that I am contributing something important to the organization
and other people

6 The Skills of the Excellent Trainer

In the last chapter we discussed ways of developing our personal qualities so as to lay the foundation for excellence as a trainer. In this chapter we will consider some of the skills required of an excellent trainer and ways of developing them further. The skills we will examine are those required for enabling learning – that is, the skills of how we train.

I am assuming that we are not, on the whole, intending to start these skills from scratch – we are not new trainers, we are enhancing the skills we already have. Some of what I cover will be merely useful reminders to you, other parts will be interesting possibilities to experiment with, and other parts you will discard as not suiting your style.

Above all, as trainers we should be comfortable with how we train because discomfort on our part is picked up by those we train and has a negative effect on their learning: discrimination is therefore needed in the way we develop our skills. Yet it is important that we extend our comfort zone, so that we are continually developing our skills as trainers and become more comfortable with experimenting with the unfamiliar. The useful beliefs we have considered and the development of our personal qualities can help us to attain this comfort. We can also find ways of developing our skills which help to make us feel safe in experimenting. NLP is particularly useful for this as it has its own built-in safety-nets and calls on our own experience so powerfully.

So let's begin by identifying the vital skills we need to be an excellent trainer and examining ways in which we can develop these skills further.

Facilitating learning and development

In every situation you face, professionally, there is the opportunity to

75

facilitate. It is the fundamental skill of training. All of us already practise this skill, although we may not always identify it as such. When we extend its conscious application to the whole process we go through when training, we significantly enhance the learning potential of the training for both ourselves and the trainee(s).

The context

To facilitate is to make easy, and this requires, first, an ability to stand away from the immediate situation and put it into a wider context.

Most providers of mortgages now have packs for potential house purchasers which go through the different stages of the process of buying a house, with checklists and guidance on timing. These packs put getting a mortgage into a wider context to facilitate the process for the purchaser. Similarly, as a facilitator of learning, we need to start by considering the wider context by stepping back from the immediate situation and asking what background and reference points will provide this context. We need, first, to know about the context and, second, to contextualize it for the learner. The context for learning may include:

- societal history and developments;
- organizational history and developments;
- departmental history and developments;
- training history and developments;
- group history and developments;
- individual history and developments.

It is important, therefore, that we keep ourselves as informed as possible about the whole context and we do that in a general sense by continually updating our awareness of developments in society, in workplaces in general and in our own professional field.

Within the specific organizational context we read the newsletters and annual reports and we ask questions to find out more: 'When did this organization begin to...'; 'What have you done already?'; 'What has been happening up till now?' It is both helpful and reassuring for the trainee(s) to realize that you are aware of and interested in the general context of the particular development because:

- it reminds them to put it into context;
- it reassures them that you are not going to treat them like a blank piece of paper;
- your awareness of a larger context can help them to feel that it's not just them – other organizations/individuals have similar issues;

- it makes them feel that you can work with them relevantly – your awareness of context will guide you to offer viable and realistic ideas.

Awareness of the context in general is not enough, though. We also need to know what exactly the learning or development is intended to achieve: of what longer-term process it is a part and what part of that process is it.

In the past, training has been used more as a one-off 'repair' to meet an immediate need rather than set into the context of continuous development. What has been called 'facilitation' has also tended to be used in this way. When we ask of what longer-term process of development this particular situation is a part we are encouraging others to view it as part of a continuous process rather than something separate. When we ask what part of the process it is, we put training back into the context of continuous learning and remind others that a separate training event is not enough on its own to embed development and make effective change.

The outcomes

Once we have established the context of the facilitation we have a more informed perspective for clarifying the intention and outcomes of the facilitation. Simple questions will enable us to do this:

- 'What is the facilitation for?';
- 'What will be the results?';
- 'What will be the effect?'.

The response to the first question gives us the intention of the facilitation. This will probably be expressed in terms such as: to enable; to increase understanding of; to encourage; to support; to reinforce. Two examples might be:

1. To enable participants to identify for themselves how the change in working practice will be of benefit to both themselves and their customers. To begin to encourage them to identify how they can play a part in developing the best of good practice in customer service.
2. To reinforce the message that managers are also now coaches, and to help develop the skills required to coach effectively.

The responses to the other two questions will give us the outcomes in the fullest sense: what people will have at the end of the facilitation and how they will be able to apply it back in the workplace. Examples of outcomes are that by the end of the training participants will:

- have strategies for helping themselves and each other to make the new working practices more effective;
- be aware of how the team approach can be of benefit to them;
- know how to create for themselves a positive attitude towards their work, their colleagues and their customers;
- recognize the importance and value of coaching as part of their role;
- be able to use simple coaching techniques effectively with their staff.

These outcomes come from asking the extra questions of the client and help us to avoid being misled. This information is vital to us as facilitators of learning because it helps us to design a process of facilitation which will enable the outcomes to be achieved.

It sounds obvious, doesn't it? Yet all too often we are misled by the way in which training is requested: 'We need something on empowerment' or 'Can you do some team building' or 'I need a sounding-board for sorting out my strategy on...'.

You can plan a superb training session on empowerment and only after the event discover that in fact they wanted something which would train people in responsible decision making. Or you can set up some useful team-building activities and only afterwards discover that they wanted to establish a team vision or to resolve a particular conflict. You can go into the session ready to be a sounding-board only to discover that what was wanted was coaching in how to develop a strategy.

By asking these simple questions we give ourselves a better chance of being effective in facilitation. We also enable those who are requesting our help to clarify for themselves what exactly they expect.

What is being facilitated

Once we have clarified the outcomes we can be clearer about what is being facilitated. NLP makes us aware that there are many levels in an individual's development, both conscious and unconscious.

While we are consciously facilitating one type of process, others may be having an effect at the same time which may or may not contribute towards what we are trying to achieve. It is worthwhile, therefore, recognizing the different aspects of development which we may facilitate. We can then consciously choose to extend our facilitation to cover those aspects which would otherwise occur unconsciously. So is what we are facilitating in the specific situation:

- a process of skills development: how to listen well, how to develop a strategy;
- a specific end result: a particular decision, a group vision;

- a plan of action: how to elicit more useful suggestions in the suggestion scheme, what to do to create a more conducive work environment;
- an improved way of working: better ways of involving people in decision making, alternative approaches to resolving conflict in a team;
- a change in attitude or belief: valuing diversity, continuous improvement; or
- a change in behaviour: managing stress, being a coach?

Notice that these are not necessarily distinct categories. By considering each in turn, we may realize that, in a particular situation, we can facilitate at two or three levels. For example, I may be facilitating a group in devising a group vision and at the same time be facilitating their identification of an improved way of working together.

By extending our awareness of the potential for facilitating development in a particular situation we enhance our effectiveness and also give added value in the work we do with others. It is a delightful surprise to a client when you say that the training you will offer will not only fulfil their requirements but will also give the added extra of team building or increased confidence.

How to facilitate

Having established what we are facilitating, we can consider how to approach it. In my experience, facilitation requires as much preparation as 'straight' training but it is of a different form. Using NLP makes it easier to do this preparation.

First, we have the outcomes, in the full NLP sense: what results will there be, i.e. what will people be able to do; and what effect will there be, i.e. how will people be. Having clarified the end result and effect, we then work backwards. So what elements need to be included for these outcomes? This can just be brainstormed.

Only then do you put the elements into some sort of order, but this order is dictated not by logic but by what will make it easier for people to achieve the outcomes. For example, you may choose to select a simple part of the process and start with that, because then they will have a sense of achievement and that will help in tackling the more difficult parts.

Then we ask the question: 'How can I make it easy for them to learn from this?' This helps to define the approach to each step of the process. It also helps to remind us as trainers that we are there to help people to learn and develop, not to prove that we are professional. For example, overhead projectors can be an aid to learning sometimes but are more often than not a switch-off for the learners.

The next question is: 'If I were the learner, what else would help me to learn from this?' This reminds us to remember what it's like to be a learner and to add to our possible approaches.

Finally, we can ask: 'And if that doesn't work, what else can I do?' This extends our choice of alternative approaches.

In this way we end up with a basic framework for the process of facilitating with a repertoire of alternative approaches. (For an example of this model of planning, see the section on preparatory stage of training, pp. 89–117.) This gives us the freedom, once we're in the situation, to notice how people are reacting and take action by doing something different if they're not learning easily. As facilitators, rather than being constrained by our programme or plan we use it as the structure from which we can concentrate on making the learning easy. So our attention is with the learner(s), monitoring what is happening with them and making adjustments where necessary to help the learning.

This process of facilitation applies to all situations. For an excellent trainer, it becomes a habit rather than something consciously thought about. As we examine different aspects of training in more detail, you will notice examples of the application of the process.

Empowerment of others

As excellent trainers, we need to know how to empower others. In the changing world of organizations, empowerment is a favourite word but it is not clear exactly what it means. As someone said to me: 'Does empowerment mean that I can decide for myself how I want to work, or that I have to do my own typing?' And maybe it means both, and many other things, depending upon the particular work context and the stage individuals have reached. As trainers we need to go back to the basics of empowerment and help people to achieve them so that they can enjoy the fruits of the particular meanings given in their organizations.

We are empowered when we recognize our ability to do something for ourselves and when we know how to use that ability appropriately. The two parts to this are vital: it's not enough to recognize that you can ride a bicycle, you also need to know on which side of the road you can cycle most safely and what the safety rules about cycle riding are, otherwise you may do harm, to yourself and others. Similarly, empowerment without responsibility and awareness is dangerous.

What is more, we need to practise being empowered. Most people who have just learnt to ride a bicycle will practise on quiet roads first, not in a busy town centre at rush hour. Empowerment is a process of gradual expansion of potential, not a one-off change. It is important, as trainers, to be aware of this, and to consciously enable the continuous development of empowerment in others.

Modelling empowerment

We have already talked about modelling – setting the example – in the qualities of an excellent trainer. Modelling is a powerful first step in empowering others because people will believe our words about empowerment only if we are also living examples ourselves. We can model this in small, yet significant ways. We can:

- look like someone who's empowered – stand straight and open, stride out while walking, and so on;
- sound like someone who's empowered – talk clearly and decisively, and take responsibility for what we say;
- if things aren't right, take action to improve them – ask for water if it is preferred to the orange squash that is offered;
- accept, but don't give in to, other viewpoints – an empowered person doesn't have to beat down the opposition and sees other viewpoints as an opportunity to extend their understanding.

By modelling the behaviour of an empowered person you offer others examples of how it works in practice and you also make it all right for them to try out some of these simple behaviours.

Waking up first stages of empowerment

Within training situations we have a great opportunity for educating people in how to be empowered with responsibility. Because we are there on the spot we can help them to make fine-tuning adjustments so that the empowerment is effective for them and others. We can also make a training environment a safe place in which to experiment with what happens so that people can practise without fearing the consequences.

First, we can help them to recognize their ability to do things for themselves. Most people have learnt to restrict themselves so well that they do not even recognize the talents they already have. Three NLP approaches in particular are useful in this regard.

Relating to previous experience

Most people feel more empowered if they can relate what is being learned to what they already know. In a more general sense they feel more empowered if they can relate what they need to do, to things they've already done.

As excellent trainers, we will look for ways of relating whatever we are training in to their previous experience. For example, when I'm training in consultancy skills and people say that they've never done consultancy, I remind them of the consultancy we do with family, friends – it's just that it is not usually called that.

If you're not sure that you can find a universally relevant previous experience you can use the technique I suggested for developing your personal qualities. Ask people to remember a time when they used similar skills in the past, and let them suggest their own examples. Remember that, even if people haven't used a similar skill before, everyone has learned something new in the past and has sometimes done that easily.

Asking useful questions

We often try to empower others by telling them what to do. This actually has the opposite effect in many cases because it gives them the message that they need to be told.

In NLP the approach is to ask rather than tell: 'What do you think would make it possible for you to...'; 'How would you tackle...'; 'What would enable you to...'. By structuring the questions carefully we can help people to produce their own solutions, which enables them to recognize their own ability.

We use 'what' or 'how' because they elicit actions, rather than 'why', which elicits reasons. We use 'would' because it implies by choice, rather than 'should' which implies by imposition, and we use 'you' to personalize the responses so that people take ownership of the action rather than saying 'they' have to do something.

Presenting the questions requires careful thought. Often, when you ask a question, people try to guess the right answer. With these questions, we should explain that there is no one right answer – in fact there may be several possible answers – and that we are genuinely asking for their views.

To support this intention, we should accept all their answers! Sometimes this may be difficult. For example, if you ask someone 'How would you tackle the unpleasant attitude of so-and-so?' and they say 'I'd kill him!', we should accept even such an extreme answer, without necessarily agreeing. You might say, 'That's one possibility. And if that's not feasible, how else could you handle it?' In my experience, by allowing and accepting the less useful answers you soon arrive at useful and constructive ones. (There is a further selection of empowering questions in the final section, pp. 193–94.)

Giving choices

The third approach which enables the development of empowerment is increasing awareness of choice.

In the first place, we can extend simple choices: 'Do you want coffee at 10.00 a.m. or 10.30 a.m.?'; 'Do you want to read this through first, or talk first and read it later?' By giving some element of control over the situation to people we empower them. However, it is important to set the parameters to the choice. 'What do you want to do next?' is not an empowering question if people don't know what they have to choose from.

Our use of questions can also encourage them to have choices. If we ask them to suggest several possible answers or strategies, and then select the one(s) they prefer, we are allowing for individual choice.

By gradually extending the number of ways in which we offer and encourage choice we enable people to accept more and more empowerment with responsibility.

Using ability appropriately

Once we have begun to give confidence to people that they do have abilities and can make choices, it is important to ensure that they know how to use these abilities appropriately.

There is nothing more disempowering than giving people confidence in their abilities and then exposing them to situations where they use them inappropriately and get put down for it in one way or another. At the other extreme, people making inappropriate decisions can be extremely disruptive to others.

As trainers, we can help people to identify how they can check out appropriateness so that they have empowerment with responsibility and also continue to extend their personal empowerment. Again NLP is useful in this process, with its emphasis on ecology and clarifying outcomes.

Ecology

Ecology is checking that an action will not throw the system out of balance. That system may be the individual, the individual in relation to others, and/or the individual in relation to the world around.

So, the first check is with the person intending to take the action and requires a simple question, 'Will I be comfortable if I do this?' This question is more usefully answered from the unconscious wisdom rather than the logical head. The quickest way of finding out that answer is by imagining yourself into the situation and checking if it feels all right. If not, there is a second question: 'What, if anything, would make me comfortable doing this?'

The next check is in relationship with others. The question here is, 'How would others affected by this action react?' If you think that their reaction would be adverse, then there is a second question: 'How, if at all, could I make that reaction a positive one?'

Last, we check the ecology of the action in a more generalized context: 'What other effects might this action have?' Again, if they are effects you don't want, there is a second question: 'What way, if any, would I change those effects to positive ones?'

This ecology check takes longer to write than to do, and is a vital reminder to us to check the possible consequences of our actions before we take them.

Let's run through an example. Someone has taken up the statement of the department head that they can personalize their immediate work environment. They have the confidence that they are so empowered and decide to bring plants from home to put on the filing cabinet.

First, the personal check: yes, that will feel all right for them. Now, others' reaction: Jean will like it but Jenny may object because she usually puts the post and urgent messages up there. What would turn that into a positive reaction? Maybe a small board for messages and post, or a basket on the desk. Or maybe just asking her if it's all right before doing it. And the boss? No problems there. Finally, other effects: all positive. So, by a simple check, this person determines how to make the action appropriate and one leading only to positive effects rather than a potential falling out with a colleague.

Clarifying outcomes

Very often when organizations empower people they don't clarify the parameters. In the example above it would not have been acceptable to personalize the office by bringing in a music player, even if that were fine with the others in the situation. But no one had said so explicitly.

By training people to clarify the outcomes expected of the action, we can enable them to avoid the disempowerment of 'No, I didn't mean that.' Part of the personal empowerment process is learning to check out for yourself what the parameters of others are by asking: 'What results, what effects do you want?' 'What choices are there?'

In the example used above, answers to these questions might have been 'I want everyone to feel more at home and comfortable in the work environment. I want them to feel as if it belongs to them. I also want it to look attractive and pleasant for anyone coming into it so that it gives the impression that we care about our environment. You can try out anything which might produce these effects so long as you bear in mind that it has to work for all of us.'

Within the training environment we can not only give people opportunities to practise empowerment with responsibility, we can also train them to use these checks once they return to the workplace.

Getting results

As excellent trainers, we need to be able to facilitate learning and to empower others, yet we also need to get results. We should avoid becoming so caught up in facilitating and empowering that we don't actually get anywhere! It is a serious criticism levelled at those trainers who pay attention to these process skills that the training gives no tangible results. The excellent trainer is effective in integrating the process and product skills together. So how do we develop our product skills?

NLP is the conscious awareness of how to make the difference to be excellent. It makes explicit what people do to make that difference. It can therefore be used as a model when we want to develop our product skills.

First, it encourages us to be explicit about the products of enhanced learning skills and empowerment which will be a part of any training we undertake. This means that we don't just enable people to learn and develop, we also point out what they have learnt about learning. We can also encourage them to notice where/how else they could use this. In coaching someone in how to present information to a meeting, for example, we may have gone through a process of deciding what information to use. Before going on to the next stage we can point out to them that they have now established an approach to decision making that suits them. We can also ask them where else they could use this approach.

Second, we can use the model of NLP in the sense of putting emphasis on usefulness and application. Whatever type of idea we are exploring in our training, we need to ensure that it leads to something useful and usable in the workplace, otherwise we may get the 'that's a good idea but it'll never work' reaction. This requires that we think through how it can be useful to the trainee(s) and what will make it usable.

To make it useful, we need relevant examples of how application of the idea could work. The learners can then visualize its application in the workplace or in their lives generally.

Making certain that it is usable requires that we ensure that it is easy to learn and to apply. If it will take much conscious effort, most people won't bother. When working with the learner directly, we need to check that they can see it as useful and to rehearse its application with them. For example, I may propose that a 15-minute informal session before a meeting is a good idea. And that it is useful because you can assess people's mood before you start, give time for people to leave behind whatever they were doing before, and perhaps find out the gossip that's going on, and because it gives people a chance to get to know each other and relate in a different way. Then I may suggest that they imagine having a similar session at the beginning of the next meeting they call. What effect would it have? And if they wanted to work better, what else could they do? I would also model the application of it by having had an informal session, with coffee, before starting the training in order to give a live example of its potential benefits and a clearer recognition of how it would work. This would also give me something to refer back to. They may then decide that the principle is good but that they would need to reduce it to ten minutes for their situation. The good idea has now become relevant and workable, and is far more likely to be used.

Conclusion

There are many other specific skills involved in the training process, which we will consider in Part III.

The three very broad skill areas of facilitating learning, empowering others and getting results, underpin our approach to training. We have considered ways of developing those skills and taking them further.

If you are unsure of your ability in any of these areas, go back to the discussion of personal beliefs and use the method proposed there for gathering evidence that you can do this. Then begin to introduce into your practice aspects of the strategies described in this chapter and build up the skill gradually.

Whatever you have recognized as being a skill you already have, affirm it in yourself, remember examples of when you have used it and use this reminder to prompt you to use it even more often. If there are strategies discussed here that you have not used, try them out before you decide they are not for you. By making just one small difference in your use of the skills of an excellent trainer, whether that be using them more often or by adding a strategy, you will enhance the quality of the work you do.

Part III

The Training Process

So far we have considered the ways in which we can enhance our personal qualities and skills to become more effective trainers in the changing world. In this part we will consider in detail the actual process of training.

We start with the preparation for training using NLP principles to develop further our preparation skills in a way which will enhance our ability to be flexible and learner-centred in our approach.

In the next chapter, we examine the implementation of training, and how awareness of stages in the process of enabling learning can enhance the effectiveness of what we do.

The final chapter in Part III deals with follow-up on training – the need to monitor the results of our training because it is the results which matter – they are what we are doing the training for. It also explores the added value which can accrue from being meticulous in our follow-up.

Throughout the section we will cover specific NLP approaches which can enable us to enhance our excellence in the training process.

There are certain areas of the training process which would usually appear in a 'how-to' book which are barely mentioned here. I have made an assumption that you already have the basic skills required. This book is about enhancing those skills to enable learners to gain added value from our training.

7 The Preparatory Stage of Training

You realize very quickly, if you study excellence, that thorough preparation significantly enhances the likelihood of success. We have all heard this message before. The difference which NLP brings to this formula is that it highlights the fact that some of the most important preparation we can do is not in the logical and rational form which we have been encouraged to use by our normal educational training but more intuitively driven preparation.

Most of us will have put many hours of careful preparation into a particular event and exhausted ourselves trying to get it as perfect as possible, with all contingencies planned for. And we may well have also experienced the disappointment of knowing that, while we ran a technically perfect session, it somehow didn't take off or inspire the participants – some essential ingredient was lacking.

We are also likely to have experienced the time when we felt as if we were flying by the seat of our pants, because we hadn't had enough time to prepare properly, yet the event turned out to be more successful than we would have dared to imagine.

NLP gives us some clues about what are the differences which make this apparently illogical difference. It is these clues and how we can consciously use them that I will concentrate on in this chapter.

The preparation required is not necessarily time consuming, but it does cover appropriately a range of preparation areas:

- checking exactly what is required;
- finding out appropriate contextual information;
- designing an initial plan;
- ensuring that the plan meets the requirements;
- filling out the content of the plan;
- designing and producing any learning aids;

- checking preparation from the learner's point of view;
- preparing yourself for implementing the training.

In this chapter, we will go through these preparatory categories and identify strategies and models from NLP which can help to enhance the usefulness of the preparation.

Checking what exactly is required

If any form of training is to be effective, there must be an agreed definition of what effectiveness means. This pays off for both trainer and learner: the learner gets what he or she wants from the training, and the trainer can prepare to a proper specification, thus enhancing the likelihood of success.

Most requests for training and facilitation are expressed in generalized terms: 'I want them to learn about empowerment'; 'We want a course on basic people management'; 'Will you facilitate a workshop on the new company vision?'; 'He needs coaching in stress management'. Even technical training requests tend to make assumptions: 'Will you train them in the use of the new computer system?' It is dangerous to assume that you know what the person means by this general request, as most trainers have found out to their cost at some time.

NLP makes us aware that we each interpret the meaning of a statement in different ways, and that we cannot assume that someone's words mean what we think they mean. We all have different life experiences which affect the way we interpret. For example, to some people challenge implies excitement and a chance to extend their skills, to others it means that it will probably be impossible for them to act, and to others it might imply the discomfort of leaving behind the familiar. Which interpretation you make will depend on how you have come to view challenges up till now, through your own experience of things called challenges and through observing other people's examples.

What makes it more complex is the fact that often the person making the request doesn't know exactly what they mean either. They only realize that it wasn't what they really wanted after the event, which is too late. For example, empowerment has been a buzz word for a while now, and the concept has been promoted as a good thing in professional journals and business management books. So, a department head asks for empowerment training for her staff. She doesn't really know exactly what it means but is prepared to accept the expert opinions that it improves staff performance. The training expert on empowerment takes the obvious enthusiasm for the training as an indicator that the effects of empowerment are known and goes ahead with a course on basic empowerment as they understand it.

When her staff begin to suggest ideas to improve the way the department runs the department head panics because she was not prepared for this effect, and only at this stage does she say that the training wasn't what she wanted. There are now three sets of dissatisfied people: the learners, who are being prevented from using their newly developed skills; the department head, who probably blames the trainer for getting it wrong; and the trainer, who in good faith did what he or she thought was required.

Even though the results may not be as extreme as in this example there is frequently a mismatch of some sort between the desired result and the actual result of training.

Use of facilitation

It is up to us as excellent trainers to increase the likelihood of the training producing desired results. This means that we will be coaching those who request training in making explicit what exactly they want. We can do this by facilitating the process of identifying the real requirement.

We need to find out:

- why they are requesting training;
- what exactly they mean by their request;
- what form they think the training will take;
- what results they want;
- what effect they want;
- what will be evidence to them that the training was successful.

In some cases we can simply ask this series of questions and we will elicit the information we need to plan to a specification. In other cases our facilitating skills may be called upon to enable those requesting training to identify this information. At this stage what matters is that we clarify exactly what they are envisaging. It is often tempting to argue or suggest something different. This is not useful if we want to be effective. We need to listen carefully to their perspective first if we want to influence it.

It is not that my ideas as a trainer are not valid – it is that I can more effectively present them if I take the time first to find out as much as possible about the other person's perspective and ways of interpreting things. Then I can present my ideas within the context of their way of seeing things; and through this be more convincing to them.

The common elements of NLP are very useful for eliciting quality information. They give us a framework to make it easy to elicit the information we need.

Rapport building

It begins with rapport. The person concerned needs to feel that we are gen-uinely interested in their opinion and respectful of their view. We need to make them feel comfortable about expressing their answers and even about admitting that they don't really know.

To achieve this we can first set our outcome in our mind: 'I want to find out exactly what x's request for training means to him or her'. We can remind ourselves that, for excellence, multiple descriptions are valuable and help to identify differences. We need at least their description, as well as our own, to begin to have a multiple description.

We can also use the NLP operating principles to prompt us to respect and value what this person can offer. They remind us that everyone has the resources they need to be wise and excellent and it is up to us to tap into that. Also, everyone makes the best choice available to them at the time, so we need to check what is governing their choice.

Others of the operating principles highlight how much we influence what happens with others – 'all behaviour is communication' for example. No doubt you will make your own selection. We can also use triggers to help us adopt a receptive, curious and non-judgemental attitude.

In these ways NLP helps us to set the right tone for the discussion and establish rapport.

Once in the situation we can enhance rapport by ensuring that we are giv-ing the message of receptivity through our physiology. It is easy to forget that our body language will betray what we are thinking and have an effect on the way the other person responds. We can be aware of this possibility, and at the same time support in ourselves a positive and receptive attitude, if we consciously adopt a body posture which matches how we are when we are in a state of rapport.

We further enhance rapport by using similar language to them. This last point is particularly important to remember when we are wanting to elicit information. It is easy to make the mistake of interpreting answers in our own language.

If the person says 'I've requested this training in empowerment because my project officers don't express their opinions or ideas in our meetings' and you translate this into 'So, the team leaders aren't assertive', you may have missed the point. Even if it's an accurate interpretation, the person will lose confidence in your understanding of them because you have changed one part into training jargon and you have used the wrong title for their staff.

On the other hand, you can increase their confidence by checking your understanding of the same statement: 'What do your project officers have to do? Are they like team leaders?'; and: 'So does that mean you would like them to say more in meetings? What would you like them to do in meetings?'

Having made the person feel comfortable in the situation, and having established a good level of rapport, we can then facilitate their thinking process to find quality answers to our questions seeking clarification.

To help them to find the answers which they may not yet have thought through, we can add two more strategies to our toolkit for this part of the process.

Evidence of success

First, we can help them to identify the evidence that would prove to them that the training had been successful:

- What would people be doing differently?
- How would they be behaving?
- What would they be saying?
- What would you observe going on?
- How would the atmosphere be different?

This imagining the desired results and effects not only helps them, it also helps us to clarify what they want. If they are still finding this hard to define, we can go on to offer examples of what might be achieved which will help them to give a more concrete definition, either because the example is similar to what they want or because it makes them realize they want something different.

As we gradually develop the definition of what they want from the training, it is essential to pay attention to their non-verbal, as well as verbal, communication. NLP is a reminder that what people say is only a small part of their communication.

If we are busy taking notes of their requirements we may miss the fact that they looked very uncomfortable when they said they wanted their staff to take decisions on their own. This may be something that they know they should say but fear the results may not be what they want. In NLP terms, the ecology is not yet right and we need to be aware of this. If we are paying attention not just to their words but also to their tone of voice and their body language, we will be able to identify more accurately their priorities, their doubts, their lip-service and their particular concerns.

Keep note taking to a minimum and attention at maximum. We can use key words to capture the essence of what they want, and then expand them into the proposals once we have the clarification. Notice, too, that by paying attention we enhance the rapport and the feeling of being understood, which again helps to facilitate the process.

The nature of the training

A further area to clarify is what form they expect the training to take. It is easy to assume that they want a course. Again, NLP reminds us that assumptions about other views are dangerous. They may have in mind some form of action learning or self-study, so it is important to check out. Even within the course framework they may envisage a workshop style or a lecture style. Of course, this area of the nature of the training is our specialism and we may well want to influence their preference, but first we need to know what it is.

If we want to influence them we can use their own desired results as our reason. This is more powerful than just saying that we know a better way. If someone asks for a talk on empowerment, I may agree that this would start people thinking about it, but suggest that, if they want their staff to take on more responsibility and use more initiative we would probably have more effect if we used a workshop approach combined with in-work projects. I would give them examples of how this would improve the results by citing precedents.

Although this approach to clarifying the request for training takes some effort, the resultant pay-offs are considerable.

The pay-offs

As trainers we are now far better equipped to plan the training to suit the needs.

- We know the evidence that will indicate success, so we know what we have to bring out in people.
- We know the language they use and can use that same language to show we have listened and understood.
- We have established rapport with the client which will make working with them easier from now on. What is more, we have increased our chances of being perceived as effective in what we do, so our expertise is valued.
- Where we feel that we want to make suggestions to improve the potential of the requested training, we have made this easier for ourselves by listening first to how they view things, so that we can make our suggestions in ways which fit in with their thinking. By expressing our ideas and suggestions in terms that make sense to them we are far more likely to have those suggestions accepted.

We have also already given added value to the person making the request.

- By paying attention and being respectful of their point of view, we have given recognition to the value of what they have to offer.
- We have enabled them to learn how to clarify exactly what they want – a valuable skill which they can use not just on other training requests but also in many other areas such as delegating tasks to others.

This approach to clarifying the results wanted may sound complicated. In my experience the time taken in the early stages of working with someone is more than offset by the time saved in ensuring that I plan my training to meet exactly the needs of the client. What is more, clients who have once experienced this form of response to a training request usually recognize its usefulness, pick up the themes and use the process themselves to clarify the request before they meet with me, so we both contribute to making this process of clarification simple and effective.

Finding out appropriate contextual information

As well as clarifying the results required, we also need to ensure that we have found out contextual information.

NLP points out the importance of ecology – the balance of the system. Any training is the introduction of a new element into the system, and we must check that it is appropriate in terms of the effect it will have. So we have the responsibility for finding out about the system. In this instance, the system may consist of:

- background information on the company;
- information on previous training and development;
- information on the individual's previous development work;
- information on future plans for company and individual.

Not all these will apply every time, so you will select those which it is useful to find out. It is relatively easy to gather the factual information and any good trainer will automatically do so.

Soft information

The added extra which enhances our excellence is the soft information. By asking questions and observing closely we can glean information on priorities, areas of certainty and uncertainty and attitudes towards training and development. Often there is a presented version of the background information and a more valuable and accurate underlying version. There may have been a series of training programmes on managing change. When you asked if they were useful, rather than if they were 'good', you are likely to hear the range of positives and negatives which reveal confidence and uncertainties. You may also glean some useful information about attitudes to training programmes as a whole – whether they are seen to be inherently useful or just one of those things you have to do to show you mean it.

This extra information enables us to understand better the way in which we may need to adjust our training to ensure that we don't create similar negatives or that we do create similar positives!

Contextualizing information

We need to be able to contextualize our training – is it part of a programme of development; a one-off; an attempt to remedy something not yet success-fully tackled; 'another initiative'; a possible choice for people from a menu of options?

By placing the training in context we can prepare more effectively and enable those taking part to see its relevance to the company and to them as individuals.

Workplace information

The other set of soft information which we can gather from this area of enquiry concerns how the workplace operates. By this I mean the often unconscious ground rules which people observe: ways of dressing; how they address each other; strict adherence to timetables or flexibility; what titles are given to roles; how different grades relate to each other; typical in-house expressions and phrases. This information tells us about the world these people operate in and enables us to fit into that world appropriately. It makes our life easier – we won't create unnecessary barriers by turning up dressed too formally or not formally enough, for example. It also means that we can cater for their unspoken requirements so that the training feels linked to the workplace world.

Sometimes we will want to deliberately break the normal patterns to achieve a particular effect. This is far more effective if we know that we are doing it and have prepared ourselves for the likely reactions. I usually arrange training rooms in a very informal way, and remove tables, which breaks norms in many organizations. By explicitly acknowledging the differ-ence to the group and explaining the intention, I can overcome the barrier which would otherwise be created.

Designing an initial plan

Once we have gathered all the relevant information we are ready to begin the planning.

If we wish to follow the pattern of excellence we will start by confirming the intention and the outcomes of the training – 'If we don't know what we want, how will we know if we have it . . . .'

Intention

The intention of the training captures both its aim and the spirit in which it will be conducted. Examples would be:

Training event intention: To give consultants the opportunity to enhance their self-management and interpersonal skills in a way which will enable them to best use the more theoretical and technical training which the other parts of the package provide by encouraging them to explore the developments which for them would make the difference.

Development process intention: To help front-line staff to identify and develop the skills they need to deal with aggressive or upset customers by reinforcing present good practice and building on it.

Outcomes

The outcomes of the training are the statement of what people will have in their toolkit by the end of it. These should be observable results at the end of the training, and relate closely to the evidence required of successful training.

It is important to clarify that a training event can only give tools, and perhaps some practice, while a development process should result in the outcomes becoming evidenced in the workplace. These outcomes must be expressed in the type of language the client used rather than training jargon. It is essential to make the client feel that they have been understood, and using their terms does that appropriately.

Training event outcomes

By the end of this training event consultants will:

- have agreed what criteria they would use to identify an excellent consultant;
- have a range of strategies to enhance their own confidence and self-esteem;

- have identified ways of building and maintaining rapport to create an ongoing professional relationship;
- know what enables them to create trust and confidence in a working relationship;
- understand and be able to use the full process of consultancy;
- have identified practical actions which they can apply to make their consultancy more effective;
- have examined the other aspects of their training and identified ways of using it in their practice.

Development process outcomes

By the end of the process, participants will:

- have reviewed their practice with customers;
- have identified the times they have handled difficult customers well and what they did to make the difference;
- have clarified what exactly they need to help them to handle difficult customers better and which behaviour they find particularly difficult;
- have found examples of the strategies they want to be able to use when dealing with customers;
- have practised and fine-tuned the methods they think will work;
- be able to use these better approaches to dealing with difficult customers in the workplace.

Methodology

Having established the intention and outcomes of the training, the next stage is to consider the methodology to be used. The question to ask ourselves is: 'If I want to achieve this combination of intention and outcomes, what approach(es) would be most effective?'

Be sure you take into account a variety of factors at this stage, using the multiple descriptions we have available from our information gathering:

- What would be our personal preference?
- What would facilitate the learning?
- What will meet the intention of the training?
- What are the client's preferred methods?
- What will suit the culture of the company?
- What is available?

We can then make a decision on the approach or approaches to be used, remembering that we may use a combination of methods to achieve optimum effectiveness. Whatever we choose, it is important to relate the choice to what the client has requested so that they have evidence that we have taken notice of their requests.

Methodology for training event

The main part of the training will take place in a workshop. The approach used will be experiential and participative, and designed to elicit from the group their collective wisdom on what would work for them in practice. The consultant will structure and facilitate the workshop, in a way which enables the participants to rapidly identify the practical actions they need to take to make a difference.

There will also be a post-workshop follow-up day to give participants a chance to try out the actions they have identified and come back with evidence of success and any queries they have. This will help to reinforce the putting into practice of the strategies.

Methodology for development process

The process will be primarily a coaching process, working with individuals on their personal requirements. This will involve one-to-one interviews and on-the-job coaching by the facilitator.

There will also be group sessions where they can share their experiences and ideas at three points in the process: after the initial interviews; when they have all identified what they think they need to develop; and after they have begun to practise different behaviours in the workplace. These group sessions will help to reinforce and support the individual coaching process.

Content

We now have the framework for the training. The pattern of excellence gives us the formula for planning the content outline. We can use the outcomes as the guidelines for the content and ask ourselves of each outcome, 'If that is what I want to achieve with them, what do I need to get there?'

Content outline for training event

The programme will include:

- definition of excellence as a consultant;
- self-assessment against criteria of excellence;
- techniques for managing one's resourcefulness;
- strategies to enhance self-confidence;

- rapport building;
- awareness of verbal and non-verbal communication;
- ways of eliciting trust and confidence in others;
- influencing with integrity;
- the process of a consultancy session;
- essential elements of negotiation;
- practical action planning;
- review of previous training and identification of ways to make it useful.

Content outline for development process

- Initial interview – to establish the individual's perception of the problem; to review with them their present practice; to identify and reinforce current good practice; to identify areas in which they want to develop their skills, with specific examples.
- First group session – to allow them to share their concerns and identify common ground; to give group reinforcement for existing good practice; to establish links to support each other through the individual coaching.
- Individual coaching – to agree the coaching process with each individual; to set a time-scale for that coaching; to implement the first stage of the coaching.
- Second group session – to share the good ideas they have suggested and learn from each other; to reinforce the ways in which they can help each other; to use each other to try out through role play the ideas they have proposed.
- Individual coaching – to support the individual as they use the strategies they have identified in the actual workplace and help them to identify adjustments if necessary.
- Third group session – to share their experience of practising these methods; to identify how they can continue to help each other to improve their ways of dealing with difficult customers; to review the whole process of development and identify any further support needed.

Notice that the outline may not be in a logical order but will provide the basic structure for the detailed planning of the content.

Ensuring that the plan meets requirements

At this stage of the planning we have produced an initial plan. Before we go any further we will find it useful to go back to the client with the plan, written either formally as a proposal or as an informal discussion document. This way we can check that we have captured the essence of what the client wanted and make any adjustments necessary.

A further step we can take at this stage to enhance the usefulness of the meeting or discussion is to ask if this plan or proposal is sufficient or appropriate for them to use in publicizing the training. This is particularly useful for a training event, as what we have produced for the person who requested it is designed to demonstrate that we have understood their request. It may need to be expressed in a different way for the learners, however. By asking the question we prompt the client to consider whether the proposal would appeal more if it were expressed in terms which relate more to the learner's perspective.

The example of a training programme for consultancy skills may be translated into a publicity handout for the event, as shown in Figure 7.1.

The Excellent Consultant

Do you want to take your skills to an even higher level? As an experienced consultant you already know what is required of you. Yet even you may wish that you could always be at your best rather than hoping that you will produce your best when it really matters.

This training event has been designed with you in mind. It will give you the opportunity to:

- find out how to bring out the best in yourself whenever you want to;
- discover new ways of enhancing your skills;
- increase your ability to deal effectively with your clients;
- ensure that you are using all the tools available to you to be successful in consultancy.

It will be fun, as well as useful. Can you afford to miss it?

Figure 7.1   Example of a publicity handout

Filling out the content of the plan

Once the initial plan has been checked with the client we can get down to the detailed planning of the training. Here again we can use the reminders of NLP to enhance our preparation.

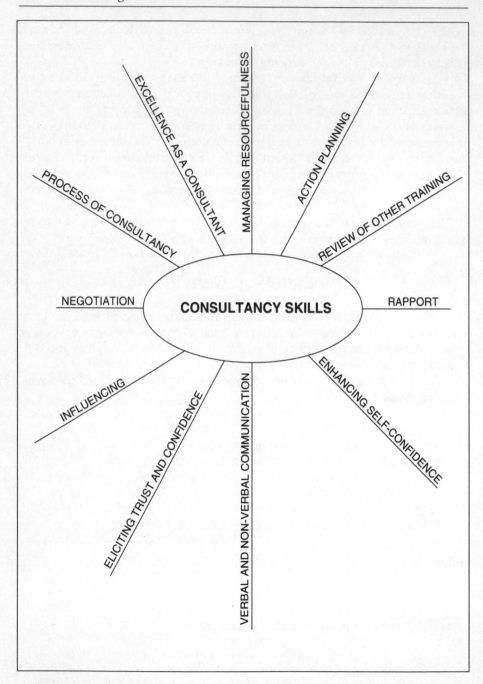

Figure 7.2   Mind map

First, we need to allow our creativity to flow. To do this we must release ourselves from the pressure of logical thought. A simple way to do that is to put down our ideas in a non-linear way. Two possible approaches to that are mind mapping and self-adhesive notes.

Mind mapping

Take a large sheet of paper, and put the theme in the middle. Now draw lines out of that theme and write the elements of the content outline on each line (see Figure 7.2).

Now stand back and identify which content area would be a useful starting point. Assess this from the perspective of the learner: what would facilitate their learning – it may not be the obvious starting point. In Figure 7.3 I have chosen to start with excellence as a consultant, because I want to set the context clearly for the participants so that they know what we are aiming for.

Now look at how you could link other elements to create a pattern for the programme which makes sense to you and to the participants. Check if there are options – there may be several routes you could take through the content, and you may be able to set up those choices to give yourself more flexibility in facilitating the learning.

You may choose to jot down your chosen order or possible options now, so you have them out of the way for the next step. Figure 7.3 shows two possible routes through the elements in my example.

Route 1	Route 2
Excellence as a consultant	Excellence as a consultant
Enhancing self-confidence	Enhancing self-confidence
Verbal and non-verbal communication	Managing own resourcefulness
Process of consultancy	Building rapport
Building rapport	Eliciting trust and confidence
Eliciting trust and confidence	Process of consultancy
Negotiation	Verbal and non-verbal communication
Managing own resourcefulness	Negotiation
Influencing	Influencing
Review of other training	Action planning
Action planning	Review of other training

Figure 7.3   Possible routes through the elements of the programme

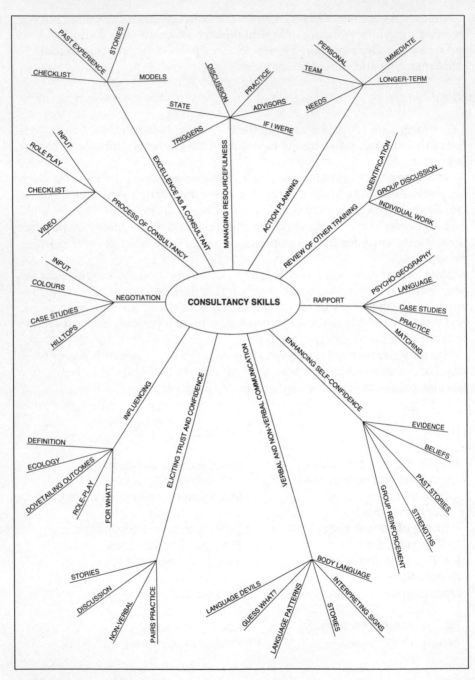

Figure 7.4   Extended mind map

These two versions of how I might link the material together reflect my intuitive thoughts on how I might make this programme both interesting and meaningful for my participants. Neither of them follows the exact pattern I would produce if I were to try and sort this material logically, so in fact I now have three different ways in which I could organize the programme and still make sense of it. This gives me flexibility of response once I have the group in front of me, and means that I do not feel tied to a particular order.

Now we can begin to add branches to each line of possible content: exercises, activities, information sessions, tasks, processes, etc. (Figure 7.4) You can slip from one area to another as ideas occur to you so that you can allow your mind to make associations across the categories. You need use keywords only to indicate what you have thought of – this is to help you in your planning, not for the consumption of others.

When you feel you have enough material, ask yourself what you could do to extend your repertoire. You could add just one item per category to increase your range of choice and encourage yourself to think outside your normal parameters.

Now take a different coloured pen and highlight or ring anything you would consider to be essential content – the core to achieve your outcomes. Next take another coloured pen and highlight or ring anything you would enjoy having in the programme. These elements are ones which will motivate and enthuse you, and including them helps you to give of your best. We all work better when we're doing things we enjoy.

Self-adhesive notes

As an alternative to mind mapping you could use self-adhesive notes for this part of the preparation.

Put the basic elements of the content outline on separate self-adhesive notes and stick them on a table or wall. Now move them around to identify possible order(s) of content until you've found one you're happy with. Record that.

Next, stick up each of these notes as the heading of a group and begin to put activities, exercises, tasks, presentations, etc. on separate notes and cluster them under the relevant heading. As with mind mapping, when you think you've finished, find a few more.

Now select out essential elements and group them under each heading. Then select favourites and cluster those under each heading.

What you now have is the basis of a training programme, with a core content, a repertoire of alternative strategies for filling out the detail, and a preferred choice out of that repertoire. You can write these on a sheet of paper if you wish.

Developing usable material

The more of this possible content you have developed into usable material, the more choice of strategies you have for facilitating the process of your learners. Developing it into usable material means some or all of the following:

- planning activities;
- planning how you will introduce them;
- planning how you will link them;
- working out what you need to support the material.

Planning activities

When planning activities remember the perspective of the learners. What will make it easy for them to learn from it and what will make this activity relevant for them?

There are many descriptions of different learning styles and we can easily become confused by trying to cater for all the possible varieties. NLP offers an alternative description which is relatively simple. People learn best when they are relaxed and enjoying themselves. This is evidenced by our own experience of learning but frequently counteracted by how we've been taught! So how can we set up the activity to have some fun in it? If there is permission for laughter, permission for a 'silly idea', permission to talk to other people, these all introduce some lightness into the activity.

If there is pressure to get the right answer, we lose the relaxed atmosphere – it reminds people of school and exams, if only unconsciously, and they react as they did to these. In many activities there is no right answer – you may be asking for opinions, ideas, discussion or conclusions. In some activities there will be a right way, but we can use the NLP presupposition 'There is no failure, only feedback' to release the pressure. Getting it wrong can be more useful than getting it right because it helps to identify what makes the difference. For example, I have asked participants to choose a topic they disagree on and try to influence the others' opinion. When they don't succeed in influencing the other person we have a useful starting-point for exploring what would make the difference and can use feedback from the other person to help identify what would be convincing. When one side does succeed in influencing the other, both sides are usually aware of what made the difference.

Another NLP presupposition which is useful in planning activities is 'We already have all the resources we need to be wise and excellent.' If we can plan activities which enable people to tap into their own wisdom and produce their own answers we are facilitating their learning and at the same time giving them ownership of the learning. By asking questions rather than giving answers we give people the opportunity to find their own solutions.

If we structure the questions thoughtfully we can elicit a best practice version which is more effective than anything we could tell them. I may say, for example, 'I have just told you about the new procedures for staff appraisal. In small groups, discuss these procedures and identify what we could do to make them work effectively. Find as many strategies as you can. When you have done that, choose the three strategies which you as a group believe would make the most difference and give your reasons.'

In my experience, asking for all the answers the group can think of results in:

- going beyond the dominant idea, whether that is a dominant person's idea or the way things have worked until now;
- an expansion of the individual's perspective through others' ideas.

I find that when they have a wider choice of ideas there is a remarkable consistency in people's collective wisdom. They know what will work best and, although they are surprised when the small groups feed back their choice of most effective strategies to discover they have all come to similar conclusions, I have come to expect that. What is more, they are far more likely to act on their conclusions since they have thought of them for themselves rather than being told. The 'expert' viewpoint can then be offered as reinforcement and support for their wisdom instead of as an imposed right answer.

NLP research uncovered the fact that we all have a preference for receiving and processing information through one of three channels: visually, auditorily or kinaesthetically. Visual preference means we like to see or visualize information, auditory preference means we like to listen to it and kinaesthetic preference means we like to get the feel of it or experience it.

This difference is illustrated by the different ways people prefer to be given directions to a location. Some people like a map – visual; some people like verbal instructions like a list of directions, turn left, go straight on – auditory; some people like a description of what it's like to drive the route: 'this is a narrow country lane where you have to go slowly, but when you reach the motorway you can put your foot down' – kinaesthetic.

When planning activities we need to cater for these different preferences to facilitate learning. By offering information to suit all three preferences we are likely to make it easier for everyone to learn. Notice that good trainers often do this unconsciously anyway. NLP simply reminds us to check that we have covered all three.

When introducing new procedures for staff appraisal I may, for example:

- produce a simple checklist of procedures as a handout to cater for visual and auditory preferences (the visual can see it, the auditory can read it to themselves);
- talk through the procedures, giving examples of what will happen (the auditory will listen, the kinaesthetic will begin to get a feel for it);
- demonstrate by role-play or video a section of the procedure (the visual will watch, the kinaesthetic will experience it).

Planning how to introduce activities

When we are creating our training plan it is obvious to us that a particular activity will be useful. It may not be obvious from the participants' point of view however. To increase the effectiveness of the activity we need to ensure that its purpose, intention and outcomes are clearly expressed and that they make sense for the learner.

When introducing the group activity on procedures for appraisal, I may suggest: 'This is an opportunity to consider how these procedures can be put into practice effectively and to propose ways of making them work. We all know that procedures alone are not enough, it's how we do things that makes the difference. We want to use your experience to help us to identify what will make the difference with these procedures. The proposals you produce will be used to help us all to implement best practice.'

Sometimes an anecdote or story in the introduction can help to make the activity relevant. For example, when introducing a role-play activity to try out a particular aspect of skill development, it helps to tell a personal story about hearing of a technique and trying it out for the first time in the workplace, without the chance to practise first in a safe environment and to describe the consequent feelings or results. This makes sense of role-play: it's not artificial, it's having a practice run. It also has the added value of letting participants know that you don't always get everything right and so increasing the sense of safety in having a go.

Give instructions for an activity very clearly. All trainers have experienced the frustration of setting up an activity and then realizing that people weren't doing what you wanted them to do. Again, we need to consider the instructions from the participants' point of view and to make explicit:

- what I want discussed, considered, undertaken;
- how long for;
- what I want as a result, or feedback, and in what form;
- what specific steps are to be taken in the process.

If the instruction is complex, either break it down into stages and give the next part when the first part is completed, or have a written checklist that people can refer back to.

Finally, when introducing an activity, give explicit parameters and permissions around the process such as:

- you must have at least five different strategies;
- spelling doesn't matter in the feedback;
- if you finish early, you can have a cup of coffee;
- everyone's ideas are to be treated with respect;
- you're allowed to laugh.

Planning how to link activities

Explain how the activities build on one another or relate to each other and to the learning outcomes of the training. Using the same approach as when introducing activities, make the activities relevant from the learners' viewpoint and continue to explain how they contribute to the learning process.

This is particularly important when we are not approaching the training in a linear way. Remember to say such things as:

- 'This is an alternative way of considering this issue';
- 'This activity will reinforce the learning about behaviour we considered yesterday';
- 'This activity continues the skills we explored this morning and takes them one stage further'.

Working out what you need to support the material

As you plan the specific activities you can identify ways of enhancing the effectiveness of the learning and list them as reminders to yourself. It is normal practice to identify learning aids, such as overhead projector slides, handouts, etc. The question is, 'what else would support the effectiveness of this material?'

We can look at three areas: environmental, behavioural and additional material.

Environmental   Apart from the obvious – have I got enough flip-charts and felt pens for the number of small groups; is there enough quiet space for the small-group discussions – we can often enhance the effect by thinking about other environmental issues.

- Is there anything I can put on the wall or in the room which will reinforce the message?
- How is the room furnished and arranged, and can I improve that for the purpose of this activity?

Behavioural   This area relates to the manner in which we want the activity carried out. It reminds us that we set the tone by how we present the material, and to consider that tone:

- Do I want participants to be creative, concentrated, have some fun, be sympathetic with each other, run to a strict timetable, etc.?
- How can I set that particular tone to the activity?

Additional material   This is a reminder to check if a story, a picture, an example, a quote, would enhance the effectiveness of the message. It may not be an essential learning aid but may be a useful reinforcement or a way of drawing attention to the topic. When I talk about using reminders to make yourself feel all right, it is useful to be able to show the group some of my personal reminders and explain their use. And a discussion about competitors had more direct impact when the trainer produced some of the competitors' advertisements to illustrate some of the points being made.

Once I have filled out the content of my plan and made it usable, I can make my final preferred selection of material for the programme. I have planned my core content, I have options for other material and I can select the material that I want to develop further with learning aids from that stockpile.

Designing and producing learning aids

There are three important points to consider when designing and producing learning aids:

- catering for visual, auditory and kinaesthetic preferences;
- the facilitation of learning;
- relevance to the normal context of the learner.

Catering for different preferences

We have already discussed this under preparing the training activity. If all your learning aids are OHP slides and handouts, you have not catered for the kinaesthetic.

The kinaesthetic preference gives us the opportunity to be creative in producing learning aids, as people with this preference like to touch things and have them physically present.

I was once running a workshop on dealing with young people and brought in live representatives of a variety of subcultures. They were each willing to talk about their subculture and why they were a part of it, and to answer questions. The learners could see them, hear them, experience being with them and even touch them!

The facilitation of learning

When we plan to design and produce a learning aid, the learners' perspective should be considered: will this actually make learning easier for them? Some so-called aids to learning are very elegant and well produced but they are more a representation of the cleverness of the designer than learning aids.

I find that the learners themselves are the experts in this area. When I try out a learning aid, whether a simple handout or something more complex, I ask the learners to assess its usefulness to me and tell me of any amendments or other ideas they have about what would help them in their learning.

Relevance to the normal context of the learner

This area is important, because we may be able to relate the manufacture of paper planes to teamwork but the learners may treat it as a quite separate activity from their normal context.

Where possible we need to link aids to learning to the context we want people to use the learning in. Again, we can be imaginative in this. I have seen Lego used with apprentice bricklayers to great effect; I used macrame to exemplify the knotty problems which managers have to deal with and communicate about. What matters is that we make explicit the links and relevance of the learning aid if they are not immediately apparent.

At a different level we can significantly enhance the effectiveness of written or verbal learning aids if we just fine-tune the language to match that of the learners' normal context. Sometimes this means using the jargon of their business, sometimes it means taking a quote from a work-related book, sometimes it means creating an example or story which is based in their workplace context or in one similar to it.

Remember that learning aids are only worthwhile if they give an added dimension to the potential learning for the learner. Often it is the simple and directly relevant ones which have most impact, although it may be the one that was most complicated to produce which pleases the trainer most!

Checking preparation from the learner's point of view

When discussing preparation I have always emphasized the learner's perspective. Our primary purpose is to facilitate learning, so we need to check continuously that what we are preparing will make sense to the learner. Once we have completed the preparation of the detailed content, we have to stand back and look at the whole package from the learner's perspective.

- Does it make sense as a whole?
- Do the pieces fit together effectively?
- Does the process cater for the involvement and empowerment of the learner?

We must ensure that there is variety of approach to keep them interested and that there are plenty of opportunities to involve them. Information needs to be given in small chunks, with time to reflect on it and apply it, so that it is properly absorbed.

We should also allow for the ebb and flow of learning by varying the pace, doing something more light-hearted or easier after something which requires concentration or effort. We can allow spaces for reflection – an extra break or a short walk, perhaps. We can also put in spaces for informal chatter where participants can relax, get to know each other better and thereby enhance the way they work together on the tasks.

It is very tempting to try to put in everything you can think of which might contribute to the learning. Remember that what we want is for the learning to be effective. There is a limit to how much can be absorbed and applied at one time, and it is better to allow for this than to push the pace and lose the learning.

Where we have a wealth of material we can use it to increase our options in the training situation. It gives us alternatives to use if one approach isn't working or if something has gone far more quickly than expected.

We have considered in some detail ways of enhancing the preparation of your training. Many of these may already be part of your practice some of the time. However, awareness of what makes the difference can enable us to improve the effectiveness of our training preparation in the areas where it doesn't always work so well. It may be that you are happy with the way you do your preparation. What these ideas may offer is an alternative which could be useful in certain types of preparation or just something to experiment with when you have some spare time. I do not suggest that this is the only way to prepare effectively, only that it is an easy and fun way to tap into our own best ideas and turn them into effective training.

Preparing yourself for implementing the training

Any experienced trainer will be accustomed to engaging in thorough preparation of material. One final area of preparation which we often neglect is the preparation of ourselves for doing the training. However well prepared the material is, if we are not in the right mood we cannot make the best use of it.

NLP helps us to remember how important our own physical and mental state is, if we want to be excellent. We want to be able to call on our best performance, to give added value to the material. After all, we are the most important learning aid in the process.

Techniques for self-preparation

There are many ways we can prepare ourselves for training. You may already use some of them, some you may use unconsciously some of the time. By being conscious of a range of strategies we can use, we can choose which ones we believe will help us to achieve our optimum as trainers in any particular situation.

Clearing your mind

When we lead busy lives, we often drag residue from previous situations into the training. We may have been in a complex meeting, or just stuck in a traffic jam – whatever it is we were doing beforehand will have an effect on our performance in the training. We therefore need to spend a few moments tidying up so that we leave any negative effects behind.

Our minds are very responsive to a conscious, ritualized clearing, but we need to know how to do it effectively. Telling ourselves to stop thinking about something doesn't work. What does work is an imaginary sorting of whatever is left over in our minds. Imagine your thoughts are pieces of paper. Take those parts of your thoughts which are useful but completed and imagine yourself filing them away in the relevant file. Take those parts of your thoughts which you will need to deal with later and imagine yourself putting them in the pending tray, clearly highlighted to mark where you're up to. Take those parts of your thoughts which need to be acted on, and imagine them going into the time-slots when you will act on them. Finally, take those thoughts which have no value or usefulness and imagine putting them in the waste-bin.

This works, even if you don't identify the thoughts separately. You can just imagine that you are sorting them and that you have the four piles without knowing specifically what is in each pile.

You now have a clear head, ready for the training.

Setting up your mind

Having tidied up and cleared your mind of the thoughts which belong to another context, set up your mind to support you in this training context.

Think about your general intention in this training and the outcomes you want, to set the context. Just reading these in your training plan will help you to create unconsciously the context in which they will happen.

Now tell yourself how you want to be in this context, for example: 'I want to be relaxed and comfortable with my material'; 'I want to notice the learners' reactions'.

Add to that some expectations you have of the learners. By telling ourselves specifically what we expect we are more likely to then automatically elicit just that – for example: 'I want the learner to be interested'; 'I want the learner to be friendly'.

You have now instilled in your mind the expectations you have of yourself and of the learners, and experience tells us that we are very good at self-fulfilling prophesies.

Reminding yourself of evidence of excellence

As you tell yourself how you want to be, and how you want the learners to be, use those words to prompt yourself to remember previous moments of excellence in your training. See, hear and feel again what was happening in that excellent training situation. Notice how you were physically, what you sounded like, what your facial expression was. Notice what the learners were like, what the general atmosphere was like.

This remembering helps us to set ourselves up for a repeat of our excellence.

Rehearsing the training

Many trainers practise their lines with a new programme. Excellent people rehearse the whole scene in their imagination. This is not a logical process but rather a rapid run-through to note what makes the difference and to set up our unconscious to help us achieve the self-fulfilling prophecy.

This is something we know we are able to do but most of us have used it primarily to predict worst-case scenarios. We are pleased when we predict something which actually comes into being, and we can say that we 'knew' it would happen or, even better, we expected it and have a strategy planned to cope with it.

If this predictive ability works, why not use it for best-case scenarios? Imagine this training event being the best you have ever done. See and hear yourself giving your best, see and hear the learner(s) responding as you want them to. Get a sense of the general atmosphere. You may not get a detailed version of this training event. It may be that certain parts stand out, as if a video were on fast-forward and then slowed down for a moment so you notice some sound or something you can see or feel.

If you do notice anything in particular, then you can be sure that it is significant in helping to create the outcomes you want. It may be something seemingly trivial. I have noticed such things as where my chair is positioned, a particular phrase I am saying, an amused expression on my face, everyone chewing a sweet. By consciously putting these things into the actual event, I have found that they do affect positively what is happening.

Pay particular attention to the start and finish of the session. At the start, notice how you imagine yourself feeling, looking and sounding. Notice exactly what you do. Notice how you greet the learners. This gives you information that you can use to consciously mimic your own rehearsal and start off on the right footing.

Now notice what it's like at the end, when you have achieved the outcomes you want. How do you feel, look, sound? What are participants saying, looking like? Allow yourself to enter into that moment of delight when you know it's gone well and you have been an excellent trainer.

This imagining is as powerful in its effect on our attitude and behaviour as real-time rehearsal is. It sets us up to perform to our own best version of the training and to do so without having to make conscious effort which would distract us from paying attention to our learners.

So far we have concentrated on strategies for preparing our mental state. By changing our thinking we can change our mood, and by changing our mood we change our physical state. Alternatively, we can change our physical state and thereby change our mood and our thinking.

Posture

When you remember a time when you were performing well, or rehearse your ideal in your imagination, notice what you're like physically. We can use this information to prepare ourselves for giving of our best.

You can consciously arrange yourself physically to be how you are when you're at your best. Shake off whatever you have been wearing as your physical posture and do whatever it is that represents 'excellent trainer' to you.

Triggers

We can use specific triggers to help us achieve the physical state we want. Look through your wardrobe and select the items of clothing which help you to feel the part. It may be colours, or types or styles of clothing associated with a moment of excellence as a trainer. Even if there are constraints on what we can wear to make ourselves feel good in training we can always add something to make a difference; such as a particular tie, a pair of socks, underwear, earrings – you will identify your own.

We can also use smells as a trigger for excellence. Which perfume, after-shave or soap represents your excellence for you? Use it whenever you want to create that state.

Some people also have an object which is a trigger for them, a briefcase, a particular pen, a photo they have in their wallet, a 'lucky' totem – again, these objects will help you to recreate that state of excellence.

Comfort to start the training

Besides using the rehearsal to help us identify what makes us feel right at the beginning of the training, we can check what else helps our mood.

- Do you like to be there before everyone else?
- Do you like to arrange your papers before anyone else arrives?
- Do you want a drink or a walk before you start?
- Do you prefer to talk to people informally beforehand or to keep your distance?
- How do you want the room arranged – are there any minor adjust-ments you want to make?
- What makes you feel in control at the start of the training?

These things are more than added extras. They are the vital components of our comfort at the start of the training and help to start us off in a state of excellence. And we can ensure that they are catered for.

I assume that all these techniques for preparing yourself for training are obvious and familiar to you. When we are in the right mood we do most of them automatically. They are the unconscious strategies for self-preparation of the excellent trainer.

It helps to become aware of them consciously, however, so that we know how we can create the right mood in ourselves when it doesn't come of its own accord.

As you have read through these ideas for enhancing your preparation for training, you may have felt that to carry them out would be too time-consuming and complicated. Yet if you reassess these ideas you will probably find that they take longer to read about than they do to put into practice. What I am describing is an alternative approach which, at first may take some extra time and conscious practice but for which the pay-off, in terms of effectiveness of the training, is substantial.

When we have prepared the material and ourselves in the ways described here it is far easier to implement the training in a way which benefits the trainee. We have set ourselves up for success and can therefore pay attention to fine-tuning the training for excellent implementation.

With practice this form of preparation becomes automatic and is actually quicker than traditional preparation. We are continually building on basic patterns and structures of preparation and adding to our repertoire. Remember that it makes a difference if we just add one extra strategy to our existing preparation methods. We do not have to adopt the whole package at once.

8 The Implementation Stage

In this chapter we will consider the process of running a successful training event. We have already discussed some of the fundamental skills and qualities required to make excellent training happen. Here we will add to those areas, by examining the working of successful training.

After all the planning and preparation we are now entering into the actual learning situation. It is easy to be so enthused by your material that you just want to get on with it. However, the excellent trainer is aware that the way we start significantly affects the effectiveness of the training, and will therefore spend some time setting the tone.

Setting the tone

Establishing relationship and rapport

When people first meet they want to know who the others are, and how they tick. This applies as much to training as to any other interactive situation. If we have not had a chance to establish a relationship we do not function well. Even if we do already know each other, the reaffirmation of the human relationship is important.

Most trainers would introduce themselves to the learners and ask the learners to give their names. The excellent trainer uses this activity to begin to establish relationship. There are a variety of ways we can do this and no doubt you have your own favourites. Bear in mind the purpose behind the activity is to:

- actively learn the learners' names – addressing someone by their name makes them feel noticed and valued, so we should actively engage in paying attention to names;

- begin to establish relationship – by responding positively to each individual as they introduce themselves through body language, facial expression and anything we say, we are showing due respect for their world;
- give a group of learners a chance to find out who they are and begin to build their relationship with each other in this environment;
- encourage recognition of the value of relationship and rapport in enabling learning – by giving time to recognition of the people involved in the learning we automatically do this.

Remember that this activity has such a valuable purpose. It may be tempting to skip this stage when learners and trainers already know each other. An excellent trainer will simply adjust the activity. For example, I may ask everyone to give their name and one thing they're looking forward to, and start the round off myself. This means that if anyone is unsure of who others are they have a chance to find out without embarrassment. It also gives a chance to recognize and relate to individuals in a positive way. It is surprising how often people comment that they have heard a different side of someone they thought they knew well.

Establishing a learning state

We have discussed in detail how to set yourself up and prepare yourself to be an excellent trainer. If we want to make life even easier for ourselves it is worth taking a little time at the beginning of the training to encourage our learners to be excellent learners. To achieve this we can use strategies which help to trigger them into that state.

You can use some of the same strategies which you have used for yourself to establish the right frame of mind to be an excellent trainer. You simply have to adjust the intention from excellent trainer to excellent learner. If these methods seem too esoteric for the start of a training session, then you can adapt them and use the principles involved as the basis for a brief discussion. This way you will help people to unconsciously set themselves up to be excellent learners without making a big deal of it.

I often ask people to spend a few minutes tidying up their brains before we start. I point out that I have been thinking about other things, and they probably have too, and that a few minutes spent clearing up those thoughts, by finishing them off, writing notes and so on will allow us all to give our full attention to the present session.

I also use the following strategies to help enhance the learning state of the group or individual.

Setting ground rules

It helps to state that the intention is to make learning easy. As part of this process we can give some explicit ground rules which take the pressure off. These may include:

- *Physical comfort*   We learn best when we are physically comfortable, and this may mean changing your physical position or visiting the lavatory or getting a drink.
- *Acknowledging the ebb and flow of attention*   It is all right to fade out sometimes and to ask if you think you've missed something – and the programme is designed to allow for this ebb and flow.
- *Asking questions*   If the material doesn't make sense to you, then it is not being communicated well enough. Please ask, so we can try a different approach. And remember that if you're not sure, at least one other person is not sure too.
- *Having fun*   Laughter and light-heartedness are not just allowed, they are positively encouraged. We learn best when we're relaxed, and fun relaxes us. Just because something is important it doesn't have to be serious.

Remembering our best examples

Another way of setting the right tone for excellent learning is to ask the learners to think of times when they have enjoyed learning, and found it easy.

Most of us arrive at a training event with some expectations of what it will be like, even if we're not conscious of what they are. For many people there is an unconscious link between learning and difficulty, so they bring with them some fear of looking stupid or being put on the spot. By asking people to remember enjoyable or excellent learning, we can break that link.

I find it important to broaden the scope of learning beyond formal teaching or training situations – sadly, there are still many people who cannot find a good learning situation in those formal circumstances. It takes only a few moments to talk about having fun learning yet the pay-off can be considerable in its effect.

Ask them what would help

We may have tried to guess what would make the environment and arrangements conducive to learning. It is worth checking if anything else would help from the learner's perspective. I have had people ask if it would be all right if they sat on the floor for the training, others ask if they could move away from the window, and there have been many other requests for simple changes which make a difference to someone's ability to pay attention. It is easy to forget that people may not feel free to make these changes without permission because they are used to being constrained or distracted in a learning situation and accept that as part of what happens.

By giving examples of how people sometimes do not think of helping themselves we can also prompt them into recognizing that they can often make minor adjustments to ease their learning. For example, someone may have automatically gone to sit towards the back – old school habits die hard! – and then realized that they really want to be able to see the flip-chart or slides more easily.

Ask them to guide you in facilitating their learning

Early on in the session set the tone which confirms that this training is intended to benefit them. By giving explicit permission to them to ask for a different description if what you're offering doesn't make sense to them, you give them more control over their learning. We may need to encourage this behaviour, as learners traditionally have not felt able to question or request another approach.

I find that the NLP presupposition, 'The meaning of your communication is the response you get,' is a useful prompt for me. I tell my learners that if my message hasn't got through to them clearly, then I've not got it right yet and I would welcome some help from them in improving the way I'm communicating it. I add to that the comment that if there are no questions or requests for a different description I will worry that everyone has gone to sleep, since I know for sure that I haven't yet perfected my communication!

Once we have enhanced the learning state of the learners we have also enhanced our chance of being effective as trainers. The next step is to check that we all have a shared view of what the outcomes of the training will be. Having laid the foundation for a successful learning event, we now need to ensure that the outcomes are relevant and useful from the perspective of the learner so that they are motivated to maintain their good learning state by their expectation of what they can get out of the learning.

Sharing outcomes

In our preparation we have already thought through our intentions and outcomes for the training. We can use these as a starting-point for sharing outcomes. Check that these make sense to the learners and be prepared to offer examples or fuller descriptions if necessary. We all find it useful to have some sort of overview of what is going to happen to help us put each part in perspective.

The next step is to ask if there is anything else they want from the training. This may seem like a dangerous question – what if they want things we can't offer? In my experience this question helps to improve the training process rather than impair it.

They may ask for things which you know will occur in the training; you can therefore assure them that it will be covered. They may ask you to deal with specific issues, which can be easily introduced either as case studies or examples; you can use this as part of the material, knowing that you are thereby making the training even more relevant from their point of view. They may ask for things which you can't cover in this training: better to know and deal with this unmet expectation at the beginning than have it as feedback at the end!

Asking what they want and dealing with it involves the learners in the learning process from the start and turns our one-sided planning and preparation into a two-sided contract for learning. It is also an opportunity to reassure the learners, to find out their views and to begin to customize our overall plan to suit their needs.

Setting the tone for the training can be achieved in a relatively short period of time and will significantly affect the rest of the training process. Throughout these initial stages of the training process we are setting up how the learners will approach the actual training.

As well as the conscious awareness that we want the training to be effective, at an unconscious level the learners will have noted that:

- the approach is positively oriented;
- they have an active role in the process;
- they are valued;
- they can control the learning.

We should maintain those underlying messages throughout the training process. And the most important way in which we do that will be through the manner in which we train. We have already explored the skills and qualities of an excellent trainer: what they are, how to develop them and how they affect the practice. In doing this we covered many of the fundamentals which make a difference to the approach we take to the actual training. The emphasis has been on how we can facilitate the learning for the learner. Besides those aspects of facilitation which apply generally to all aspects of training, there are other specific ways in which we can enhance the effectiveness of what we are doing in the face-to-face training which complement and add to what we have already covered. We will now consider a selection of those.

Paying attention to what is happening

As a facilitator of learning, it is our responsibility to monitor constantly how the learning is progressing. Notice that this is a shift from the traditional monitoring of whether we are getting through all our material. It means that our attention is with the learner and we adjust our material to suit their needs.

NLP reminds us that the attention levels we commonly use give us only limited information. We may pick up factual information – what people say – and some very obvious non-verbal information – such as if someone is consistently looking away – but we miss consciously the small clues which can help us to adjust what we are doing before it reaches crisis point.

So, when we are paying attention, we should use our whole selves – our:

- ears – to hear the conscious message being given;
- 'inner' ear – to hear the hesitations, enthusiasms, hidden questions;
- eyes – to notice whether the body language matches the verbal message;
- guts – to pick up those messages that are less obviously expressed;
- hearts – to ensure that we respect and appreciate a person's viewpoint, and use sympathetically the messages we pick up.

If you want to use this multi-level attention it requires only that you give yourself that message clearly and positively. Your unconscious will then switch it on automatically for you.

From this form of attention we gain information that means that we never have to ask the question 'Have you understood?' We sense when an extra example would be useful, when a different way of expressing something would help, when we need to slow down or speed up. And by responding accordingly we avoid ever reaching the point of losing our learners.

There are a variety of ways in which we can apply this attention.

Giving information

Whenever we are giving information we should notice the learners reactions so that we can fine-tune to facilitate their learning. It is easy to be swept along by the momentum of your input and miss the fact that you left your learner several paragraphs behind.

This means that we should give our complete attention. We all know that it is not enough to just ask 'Have you understood?' every so often. And we all know that there is a danger that our information will not be absorbed as we would like it to be. We may try to get it right logically, using, for example, the theory that people have an attention span of ten minutes so we mustn't give solid input for longer than that. In my experience this is a generalization which is frequently proved wrong, and too many breaks in the information can be as frustrating for the learner as too few.

By paying attention to what is happening with the learners, noticing slight shifts in concentration or the tiny signs of some puzzlement, we can perfectly gear our giving of information to their needs in the particular context.

During activities

When we have set up an activity for the learners we can take the opportunity of not being centre stage to pay attention from a different angle. We have an opportunity to monitor from a more relaxed position – we are not trying to hold their attention at the same time.

NLP emphasizes the importance of gathering multiple descriptions to fill out your own perspective. There are three basic perceptual positions we can adopt to increase our awareness of what is happening.

1. *Our own viewpoint*   Notice how the learners are responding to the activity. Are they engaged? Are they finding it easy to follow your instructions? Are they enjoying it?
2. *The learner's viewpoint*   Imagine yourself as the learner. Is this all making sense to you? Are you feeling in control? Are you learning?
3. *The observer's viewpoint*   Step back a little and notice the overall atmosphere and reactions. Is the atmosphere buzzing? Do people look as if they're comfortable? What is happening here?

We also get a perspective on what is happening overall, not just what is happening during the activity.

By gathering information from these different perspectives we can often fine-tune to enhance the effectiveness of the training, for example by:

- adjusting the break time;
- adding some positive feedback for the learner who is feeling a little unsure;
- adding in an extra linked activity to reinforce the message;
- lightening the atmosphere by adding in a fun activity;
- speeding up the next section because they have clearly got this message;
- restating the relevance and usefulness of this activity in relation to the overall outcome.

Monitoring activities

As well as continuous monitoring throughout the training, it is valuable to put in specific monitoring activities at regular intervals. This gives the learners an opportunity to notice for themselves what is happening. It is an important part of the learning process to reflect and consider consciously where we have reached in our own learning. It is also part of the development of the skill of controlling our learning. As trainers, we get a chance to check that we have been interpreting accurately, in our monitoring.

These activities can be brief, just taking the temperature of the moment, through to quite lengthy, structured, feedback sessions. For example, I may just ask each member of the group to comment on the session so far. Or I may ask them to form small groups and produce a checklist of learning points so far. We would then compare these checklists and discuss them as a group.

From this explicit monitoring of where learners are up to, we can take information which helps us to fine-tune the programme. We may need to speed up or slow down, to introduce some simple activity to give a feeling of getting somewhere, or to stop and find the good learning state again.

Modelling

Paying attention

We have already discussed the importance of modelling for the learner. By giving this level of attention to the learning process we are also modelling good practice for the learners. We are consciously engaging them in their own learning development, encouraging them to reflect, to notice what and how they are learning and to express any need they may have for something different. In this way they become aware that it is important to notice how the learning is going, not just what has been learnt, and that they can control the process.

We are also modelling the good practice of paying full attention when required. This can be used by participants in a variety of contexts and is worth drawing to their conscious attention. You can even take them through the five levels of attention and ask them to try out paying this type of attention to each other as part of their activities. I use this in programmes involving listening skills and in any which have to do with interpersonal skills.

Effective communication

By paying full attention we are setting an example of a form of effective communication which learners can use in other work situations. The message they take away with them is that it is the responsibility of the giver of information to ensure that the receiver of information has taken the message as they intended. We also make it clear that it is all right to have another try at getting your message across.

It is not enough to just check understanding, however. We also need to ensure that we are exemplifying two other aspects of taking responsibility for communication.

Accepting other viewpoints

When we ask for feedback and it is not what we would like, we may be tempted to be defensive or dismissive. These reactions are normal, but it is important to leave them to one side. They are not useful in this context. Remember our intention: to find out what facilitates learning, and to find out what may be blocking learning so that we can do something about it.

Whatever people give as feedback gives us the information we are asking for: their perspective on what's happening. So we need to accept and value their viewpoint. By doing this we are setting the example of recognizing that everyone has their own interpretation of a situation and that their interpretation is valid. By finding out their interpretation we can work with it rather than trying to force them out of it or ignore it.

Acting on feedback

Once we have been given information on what is happening, it is essential to demonstrate that we have taken notice of it. The information is useful and valued only if it is acted on. This means that we will relate whatever we do next in the training to the comments in the feedback by saying, for example:

- 'I notice that a number of you feel the pace is rather slow. Let's speed it up a bit with this summary activity'; or
- 'I notice that there is some confusion over the relevance of x. It was intended to develop this skill, and maybe we need to look specifically at what would help you to experience that development'; or
- 'I notice that several of you are not sure if you have grasped the point of x. We will return to that theme this afternoon through a different activity, and you can let me know if that has made it easier to understand'.

We may not make such a statement at the time of the feedback but may refer back to it as we act on it in subsequent parts of the training. What matters is that we exemplify the good practice of demonstrating that we have taken notice of what will make a difference to these learners.

Empowerment

Through these responses we are also modelling empowerment of the individual. By giving value to, and responding to, the individual's perspective we give them the entitlement to have an influence on their own learning. Consciously or not, the group will notice the positive effect this has on them and will begin to treat each other in a similar way.

The theme of empowering the individual can be reinforced in other ways. As well as encouraging and taking notice of feedback we can set up activities in a way which implicitly empowers the individual.

Finding solutions

We can ensure that the activities are designed to emphasize the finding of solutions rather than to analyse problems. This is a fundamental NLP approach. If something is wrong, it is more useful to give energy and attention to working out what would make it better, than to spend time analysing what is wrong. This emphasis in the activities empowers in two ways – by:

- implicitly assuming that the individual can make a positive difference to the problem, that they are not dependent on others changing things;
- assuming that the individual, rather than some detached expert, will have the best solutions to the problems they encounter.

Even if the learners require some extra information to increase the likelihood of their identifying possible solutions we can still use the same approach. When I am training in appraisal skills, I may give inputs and activities which lay out the various skills and processes required for effective appraisal. I can then ask the group to assess the information they have gathered and from it to formulate their own strategies for handling an appraisal interview effectively or for overcoming the obstacles they can identify to running an effective appraisal interview.

We enhance the empowerment inherent in this approach to activities if we take their ideas and use them as the handouts for the activity. The traditional approach to solutions has been to have the 'right' answers prepared on a handout, and for these 'right answers' to be what the leading theorists say or the accepted technically correct procedures and actions. By asking the group to discuss their solutions and then giving them such a handout we can easily disempower them. On the other hand, by taking their ideas, in their own language, and feeding them back to them as handouts post course, we can powerfully reinforce the value and usefulness of their solutions.

In my experience, the group usually suggests answers which are at least as good as any expert's and, furthermore, they are far more likely to use the ideas in their work practice when they have thought of them for themselves.

Building on strengths

The empowerment of individuals begins with recognition of the capabilities and qualities they already have. That recognition is easily given within the training context, yet it is also easily forgotten. By asking learners to identify what they already have which will help them to achieve the new learning we give them the opportunity to identify the base from which they are building. Most people, for example, have managed change in their personal lives: leaving home, getting married, changing jobs and/or location. These experiences will have given them some useful skills for managing change in an organizational context. By identifying what they have learned, we have the basis for exploring further learning on managing change.

In a more general sense, everyone has learned something new. By showing them how they have developed some learning skills already we make it easier for them to tackle the new learning we want to explore with them.

When we start with what people already have, and then develop and build from there, we make a significant difference to how they approach the learning:

- The learning is no longer so worrying because they know they have a foundation on which to build rather than starting from scratch.
- By giving value to what they already have, we automatically create in them a more positive state.
- We avoid the problems and frustrations caused by people feeling as if their existing skills are being ignored and they are being treated like a blank sheet of paper.

Flexibility

One of the qualities of an excellent individual is flexibility. It features as one of the NLP operating principles and is built in to many of the approaches we have looked at so far. It is a vital part of the empowerment of individuals, and again is a quality we can model through our approach to training.

It is useful, however, to consider some deliberate reinforcement, as most of us have been educated to look for the 'right' answer. Despite the fact that our life experience clearly evidences that there are few areas where there is only one right answer, the unconscious effect of our formal schooling remains.

As excellent trainers we demonstrate flexibility by having more than one way of getting the message across and by being prepared to use alternatives when our first choice isn't having the effect we want.

We also model flexibility through our willingness to accept different points of view when we ask for feedback. We can take this further by actively encouraging our learners to come up with a variety of alternative strategies for dealing with an issue. By asking for as many different ways as they can think of to solve a problem, and by accepting all the ideas as having validity in the appropriate context, we help them to recognize the value of having a repertoire of responses or reactions.

We can also enhance their awareness of the value of flexibility by using a variety of ways of forming them into small groups: pairs, threes and fours; with people you know, people you don't know, the person beside you, someone on the other side of the room. They then have to adapt to working with different characters and personalities and experience the variety of ways of working together.

In my experience this is a feature of the training which people value highly. They discover that they enjoy the mixing, once they have got used to the idea, and it helps them to learn how to break down artificial barriers which have often been created only in their own heads. This learning has clear benefits for when they are back in the workplace. They feel more able to relate easily with the people who were also on the programme, and they also realize that other people may be equally approachable given half a chance.

In this chapter I have used the group training session as the basis for my discussion. All the points made can be applied equally well to one-to-one coaching and facilitating sessions, with very slight adjustments. I have paid attention to the ways in which we can reinforce the underlying messages of any learning and development. As an excellent trainer I will be aware of my overall role and function as well as my specific intention and outcomes in any particular piece of training. I will use every opportunity available to me to build the basics of excellence with others:

- learning how to be an excellent learner;
- being able to be effective in change;
- using the best of yourself;
- developing flexibility and empowerment;
- respecting and valuing others.

By having the learner as your focus of attention, rather than the material, you will ensure that you give this added value in all the training you undertake.

As I have said before, you are likely to have read through this and thought that some of it is useful, some of it just reminds you of what you do already and reinforces its value, and some of it may not appeal to you. Take what is useful to you. Any of it will add value to your training for the learners and also make it easier for you to get the results you want. Any difference makes a difference.

9 The Follow-up Stage

We have examined the ways in which we can enhance our training, both by the way we prepare and by the way we approach the training itself. Yet this is not the end of the story. Before we can claim that we have been successful in facilitating the learning we intended we need evidence that the learning outcomes have been fulfilled.

The excellent trainer recognizes that this is an important part of the learning process, both for them and the learners. The trainer gains feedback on the effectiveness of their approach in enabling learning which is useful in practice. The learner gains conscious awareness of their own learning and how it is useful.

There are plenty of thorough descriptions of the fundamentals of evaluation and I will not replicate them here. In this chapter we will examine how we can use the principles of NLP to increase the value of our evaluation process.

Immediate evaluation

The first part of the follow-up evaluation process is at the end of the training. Having stated our intention and outcomes at the beginning of the training, and having agreed outcomes with the learners, we now need to check to what extent those intentions and outcomes have been met within the training context. This can be done in differing degrees of detail, depending on what you want to check.

If you have been monitoring the progress of the learning throughout the implementation, this may be no more than a summary evaluation covering, for example:

- To what extent were the outcomes met? State those which were fulfilled and identify what else you needed on those we didn't meet.
- How was the intention fulfilled?
- How did the event match up to your expectations?
- State any aspects of the event you found particularly useful, and how.
- State any aspects of the event which you would have liked to be different, and in what way.
- Add any further comments you would like to make.

Thus far is normal good practice for trainers. The excellent trainers will add two further pieces to this end-of-training evaluation.

Process evaluation

As excellent trainers, we want to know not just what was learned but also what worked well in the learning process. We can use questions like:

- What did you enjoy about the training?
- What helped you to learn?
- What did you like about the approach?
- Is there anything else which would have made the learning easier for you?

From these we gain some feedback on the extent to which our approach facilitated learning. We also give the learner some awareness of what makes learning easier for them. This is information they can use to add to their learning skills from now on.

Future application

We can also encourage the learner to begin to consider how they can apply what they have learned in the workplace. NLP recognizes the importance of using our imaginations to rehearse changes in our practice. By running a video in our minds of what will happen when we put our learning into practice we both enhance its effectiveness and make ourselves ready to use it.

We can prompt learners to do this in several ways:

- Ask them to consider how they will use what they have learned – in what context, with whom, when.
- Ask them to choose a specific part of their learning and plan exactly how they will use it – what context, with whom, when.
- Ask them to think of a specific situation which they know will happen in the next few days and imagine using their learning to make a difference to that situation.

This gives them the opportunity to consider the practical effects of their learning so that they are prepared for any differences that might occur, as well as increasing the likelihood that they will actually use their learning because they have already done so in their imagination.

Follow-up evaluation

The most important evaluation of the effectiveness of training can only occur once the learners have had an opportunity to put the learning into practice. This form of evaluation can take place only some time after the training and needs to be built in as part of the training agreement so that it is recognized as important. Often it doesn't happen because no formal arrangement was made for it to occur.

The excellent trainer will want to ensure that there is some opportunity to find out whether the learning has proved to be useful in practice and can use a variety of methods to gain such information.

Follow-up workshops

By arranging a follow-up workshop or session a month or six weeks after the training, we can give added value to the evaluation. It provides an opportunity to:

- share and value applications of the learning;
- let learners encourage each other in applying the learning;
- become aware of any obstacles to applying the learning and develop strategies to deal with those obstacles with the group of learners.

This approach also reinforces the idea of continuous learning – that a training event is not the end product, merely part of a process.

Monitoring of individual learning

Where the training was on a one-to-one level the trainer can arrange to meet with the learner and follow a similar process to that of the follow-up session.

We will always start the meeting with valuing what has been used successfully. By reinforcing success we are building on strengths and encouraging the learner to use their learning even more. Being able to find a positive approach to those times when the individual states that they have not applied their learning, is particularly important.

Check that the statement is accurate

NLP is a reminder that everyone has different perceptions. We may discover that the learner is using more than he or she consciously realizes. I find that this occurs particularly with training in the softer interpersonal skills and that I can usually elicit examples of unconscious application if I accept their initial statement and then ask them to tell me what's been happening with them over the last month.

Give credit for recognition of non-application

When an individual can tell you where they didn't apply the learning, they are indicating that they are now conscious of how it can be applied. You could ask them to tell you a situation where they know they could have applied it, but didn't.

Point out to them first that this in itself constitutes learning, and then go on to extend that into increasing the likelihood of their using the learning the next time they have the opportunity. We begin by asking them to imagine what would have happened if they had applied the learning, so that they rehearse the positive benefits of its use. We then ask them to imagine their next opportunity to apply the learning and what will happen. This both reinforces the revised version they have already thought of and increases the likelihood of their actually using the learning next time.

Taking responsibility for non-application

When there is no use being made of the learning, and not even any aware-ness of where it could have been used, the learner's first reaction to being asked about it is likely to be defensive or guilty. This is not useful, for them or us, so it is important to turn that around.

If there is no use of the learning in any way then we, as trainers, must take responsibility. The NLP principle 'The meaning of your communication is the response you get' applies here. Either we didn't convey the training message successfully for this individual, or we didn't check accurately our assumptions about what training they needed.

Having taken responsibility for the failure to apply the learning, we can now ask the learner what else he or she needs for this learning to be useful.

Dealing with obstacles

There are often sticking-points in applying the learning to the work context.

The excellent trainer will encourage the learner to give information about these obstacles because they are valuable feedback about what else needs to be considered when planning similar training in the future. Set the right tone for this feedback so that the learner sees it as valuable to both you and them. We have to come past the tendency of the learner to be reluctant to admit to 'failure', either for their own self-esteem or because they want to please you.

There are two approaches you can take to dealing with obstacles:

1. Encourage the learner to think through their own solutions. Ask them questions like: 'What would make it possible for you to...?'; 'How else could you...?'. Notice that the emphasis is on what would make it work, not what is wrong.
2. Encourage the learner to identify others who have made the learning useful, and to find out by asking them what those people are doing differently. This approach reinforces the message that the fastest way to learn is to use someone who does it well as a role model.

Finally, reinforce the process of putting the new ideas into practice by asking what they are going to do as a first step.

It is very tempting to be the expert when dealing with obstacles, and to give the learners ideas. This is particularly true when the obstacles are identified after the training has taken place – we want to 'mend' the situation because we feel some responsibility for not offering the appropriate help in the first place. However, the learner is empowered more effectively if we take the alternative approaches.

Feedback from others

In addition to the evaluation of the usefulness of the learning from the learners themselves, it can be very valuable to get the perspective of others.

Remembering that in NLP multiple descriptions are identified as giving more quality information because we all have different perspectives, we can encourage the learners themselves to ask colleagues, subordinates and managers, for feedback. It is preferable for the learner to collect this feedback, as this gives them control over the process – nobody is collecting information behind their back.

I find, however, that I often receive unsolicited feedback from others who work with the learner. We must ensure that this feedback is constructive. If we are told that it hasn't been successful, then we can ask what they think would improve the learning and then suggest that they tell that to the learner. If we are told that the individual has improved their performance, we can check that the person telling us has also told the learner this. This may seem obvious, but in my experience people are more likely to have given the negative feedback than to have offered a constructive suggestion or given credit for improvement. By prompting them in this way we are continuing to fulfil our role as continuous enablers of learning, in taking the opportunity to coach in feedback skills.

Evaluation from the organization

So far we have considered only the effect of the training on the individual. NLP reminds us that whenever there is a change in one part of the system it has an effect on the whole system.

Some form of evaluation of the overall effect of the training, as well as of the effect on the individual's performance, can be very useful. This can be difficult to set up, because it requires clear criteria. It can also be difficult to identify which effects are directly related to the training and which are due to other circumstances. However, we can ensure that the desired outcomes established when the training plan was agreed include an outcome which refers to the overall effect in the organization. Then we can ask the client to look for evidence that those outcomes have been met. Examples might be: less absenteeism; more PCs being used; fewer complaints; increased productivity. These are all measurable, and it is useful to us as trainers to know if the improvements in individual performance have produced these outcomes.

There can also be softer outcomes: a better atmosphere; more willingness to accept change; improved relations with colleagues.

Asking if the organization has evidence of these outcomes being met is useful, too. We can ask: 'What have you noticed?' or 'What differences are there?' to elicit such evidence. If no general outcomes were set out to start with it can still be worth asking if they have noticed any differences in how the organization/department/team are working.

Volunteered feedback

All the forms of evaluation mentioned so far are ones which are formally asked for and managed by the trainer. If we believe in the value of information about the effectiveness of the training we will set up the possibility of learners choosing to give us feedback as well. We can give a contact place or number for learners to tell us how they have used the learning or to consult with us if they come across an obstacle.

It is important to make it very clear that we set high value on both forms of feedback because they help us to enhance our skills in training others as well as being useful to that learner. I delight in being told success stories and in being given information about obstacles I haven't previously considered as well as the opportunity to help the learner find a way past the obstacle.

In this chapter we have considered ways of enhancing the usefulness of evaluation of the training. By taking the trouble to follow through on the training we have undertaken we give ourselves the opportunity to reinforce its effectiveness through giving recognition to any improvements which have resulted. We can also become aware of aspects which haven't worked as we intended and do something to help the learner get what they wanted.

Remember that evaluation is not the end of the process either – it is the beginning of the next cycle of planning, preparation, implementation and evaluation.

From the information gathered through evaluation, we can fine-tune our training, reinforcing what works, extending the repertoire to include strategies to help with common obstacles and adding new success stories to our stock of examples and models.

Evaluation is a vital part of the process of becoming an excellent trainer, someone whose work is constantly developing, someone who is continuously learning. The time and effort spent on evaluation benefits us by making it easier for us to plan more effectively for the needs of the learners next time.

Evaluation also benefits the learner. It is part of the continuous process of encouraging them to recognize their own learning capability, and puts training firmly into the context of improvement in the workplace.

Finally, the organization is being encouraged to recognize the part that training can play in helping to develop the business as well as the importance of giving recognition to individuals for their development.

Part IV

The Developing Trainer

We have already covered many of the ways in which the trainer can develop their own skills as they go through the training process. It is easy to let our own development slip, however. Somehow we can always find other things which we need to do first, like encouraging others to develop themselves! This is true of all professions, of course. They say that the plumber is the one most likely to have a dripping tap and the counsellor to have problems which they have not resolved with their own relationships. None the less, we should give priority to our own development if we are to be excellent in what we do.

To do this requires that we find the time for it and give it precedence over other possible uses of our time. In Chapter 10, I will take this issue of time and consider ways we can create it for ourselves, since it is an important issue for most of us. The points made there may be useful reminders to you, and of course may also be useful in helping others deal with similar issues in their own roles.

In Chapter 11 we will examine more specifically what will help us to use this time we have found most effectively so that the development gains encourage us to continue the practice.

Again, in this part, I have concentrated on the extras which can give added value to our development rather than laying out the basics. You will by now recognize the themes of excellence and hopefully find it useful to be reminded of what it is that you do to make the difference when you already engage in effective self-development.

10 Time Management

How often have you heard learners say, 'This is all very well, but I haven't got the time for it?' And a part of you agrees, as all those books you haven't read and programme changes you haven't made spring to mind! It is our modern disease to be pressurized with what's already there to be done and therefore not have time to add in development.

This pressure of time is an indicator of the need to shift paradigms – we all need to learn how to work smarter, not harder. As excellent trainers, we can set the example and model a different way of approaching our workload.

First, we will clarify for ourselves what we want – to set our outcomes on time management.

Setting outcomes

As a starting point for setting outcomes on time management we would be advised to consider our ideal, the description of our life at work and at home, as it would be if we did run it the way we want to. Most of us carry this ideal in our heads anyway – it's what we use to compare with our present lifestyle and find cause for dissatisfaction!

By expressing the ideal clearly to ourselves we can identify the outcomes we want to achieve. Begin by sketching out to yourself this ideal picture. An example might be:

> I would have time to prepare myself thoroughly for training. I would be energised to give of my best in the training, because I would refresh myself beforehand. I would have space to recover my energy and to follow up on the training afterwards. I would have the time to find opportunities to continue my own development, and follow them through. I would compare notes with fellow trainers and

between us we would develop our training further. I would also spend time in the learners' workplace, noticing where I could offer something useful, and getting to know better the context they work in. I would go home at a reasonable time, leaving my work behind. I would have space and energy for fun in my home and social life. I would have time to pursue other interests.

You may choose to write down your own version of this ideal now, and as you do so, imagine it happening. Next, consider what the effects of this ideal would be, first on you, then on others. A list of effects might include:

- I would be enthusiastic in my work.
- I would have energy to spare.
- I would be able to develop my skills.
- I would be healthier.
- I would do my work more effectively.
- I would be more sociable with friends and family.
- I would offer better training.

Write your own list of effects, and as you put each one down imagine what you will be like and what others will be like as a result. See yourself and others, hear what's being said and in what tone of voice, get the sensation of how it would feel to have these effects in your life. This is a very powerful way of beginning to build the circuits in your unconscious which will help you to achieve what you want. If we can imagine it, it is possible!

Having imagined an ideal version of how you manage your time, you can now set your outcomes for improving your time management. Read again your list of the ideal version and its effects. Now select the most important aspects for you to develop (some of it may be already in place) and express them in a statement which begins: 'I want to . . .'.

There is one warning worth repeating before you do this: make sure that it is all expressed in the positive – what you want, not what you don't want – because your unconscious doesn't distinguish between dos and don'ts. Also, check that it is genuinely what you want – your unconscious doesn't respond to any attempt to force yourself to be or do something which doesn't fit properly with you.

Finding validity

To begin to use our unconscious to help us to achieve our ideal, once we have set up our outcomes, we need to ensure that we will not sabotage ourselves with our beliefs. We convince ourselves that by managing our time differently we will bring added value both to ourselves and to our work. This is easy to do when what we want fits with the norms of society. It is harder when we are setting a new model, rather than following custom and practice. When we want to become more effective in managing our time, the desire may match with many others but the practice of it is certainly not the norm.

So what is our justification of this, to ourselves and to the other people who would expect us to stay in the 'I haven't got time' syndrome? We have already considered the potential positive effects, on ourselves and on others. That provides one part of the justification – look at the consequences. We can also consider what other beliefs we have, besides the belief in positive consequences, to support us in taking action on managing our time more effectively.

Throughout this book, we have been exploring the differences between a good trainer and an excellent trainer. By going back through that material we can begin to identify our own useful beliefs. These will fall into two main categories: beliefs about how the world of training is changing, and beliefs about what constitutes an excellent trainer.

In the changing world of organizations, we all will need to shift our perceptions of how we undertake our work, and to be able to manage our own workloads as we are given more and more responsibility for our own performance. We will also come to consider our own continuous development as a vital part of our work as we recognize that change is continuous and the future unpredictable.

As trainers, we will become more and more the models and facilitators of a changed approach to work practice, and what we do ourselves will be more important than what we tell others they should do.

The excellent trainer knows that he or she is a model or exemplar for others and is at the forefront of changing working practice. We will therefore need to exemplify what working smarter, not harder, means by:

- giving value and time to preparation of material and self;
- giving value and time to reflecting on and learning from our own practice;
- giving value and time to learning from others;
- giving value and time to maintaining and building our own good state;
- giving value and time to developing ourselves as whole human beings rather than just 'work robots'.

You may wish to add to or amend this version of the validity of changing your practice in time management by writing out your own version.

Strategies for managing your time

Once we have laid the foundation for improving our time management so as to enhance our performance, we can begin to identify strategies which will help us to achieve our outcome. Using NLP principles to do this increases the likelihood of our finding what will work for us.

Taking models of excellence

NLP suggests that when we want to improve something we look for examples of best practice and use them as the basis for our own improvement.

There are many books, articles and training programmes on effective time management. We can select from these the strategies and ideas which appeal to us. There are also people who seem to have found their own ways of having time to spare for things that matter to them. It is worth questioning them to find out how they have achieved it, but it is also important to remember that they may not be consciously aware of what makes the real difference. Asking NLP-type questions helps us to obtain the information we want. We might ask:

- How do you think about time?
- How do you decide how long something will take?
- What do you tell yourself about the time you spend on your own development?
- How do you use your diary/organizer?
- What happens when someone suggests that you are not using your time as you should?
- What do you do if you don't think you have enough time?

Customizing time management skills

Because there is so much information available about how to manage your time, it is easy to get caught in the trap of trying to do what everyone else says you should do. If we want to achieve our outcome we will weigh all the strategies suggested to us against our own preferences, needs and comfort levels. If we choose strategies which we like, or which appeal to us, they are far more likely to work for us because they are the ones which fit with how we work and what stage we have reached.

Sometimes the idea is appealing, but doesn't quite fit us as an individual. We may be able to take the basis of the idea and adjust it to suit us. When I went on a course to learn to use an organizer, I liked the basic principles but the suggestions for the categories and for some of the usage didn't fit my lifestyle. Rather than reject the concept, I took the principles and adjusted the way I put them into practice to make a better fit. Consequently I am one of the minority who still uses their organizer to organize themselves rather than just as a glorified diary.

Experimenting with alternatives

When we are looking for the strategies which will help us to manage our time better it is useful to identify some alternatives and choices, rather than only one course. The advantages of this are:

- if we try something and it doesn't work, we have other possibilities lined up, so we can try again in a different way;
- at different times or in different situations we may need alternative strategies, so by having a variety we can choose the most appropriate for the context;
- when we are working on a fairly large issue, it can be helpful to use several different strategies at once to achieve a cumulative effect.

It also frees us from the likelihood of failure if we approach new strategies as an experiment, to see if it works, rather than as 'the answer'. The trouble with 'the answer' is that, if it doesn't work, we revert to old habits. Having alternatives to experiment with gives us the possibility of continuing to try different approaches out until we find one – or several – that work for us.

Identifying obstacles

When we are selecting our strategies to make a difference we can select in a more useful way if we have worked out beforehand what the obstacles are to our outcome.

Most people have some idea of what stops them from being effective in their time management. If this has not been fully thought through, however, they often find that the strategy for tackling that particular obstacle, although effective in itself, is not enough to achieve their desired outcome.

It is useful to stop and consider the different types of obstacles and then observe which ones have the strongest negative effect on you.

Obstacles in yourself

Do you have unrealistic expectations of yourself? Do you spend time worrying about what you have to do instead of doing it? Do you place low value on time spent on resourcing your state? Do you think of time as a scarce resource? Do you imagine others expect you to maintain your old habits?

What are the obstacles which you have created for yourself?

Obstacles caused by other people

Do others demand too much of you? Do others interrupt you? Do others change your priorities? Do others make you feel guilty? Do others waste your time?

What are the obstacles caused by others that you need to tackle with them?

Obstacles in the overall system

Is your job specification narrow and inflexible? Is your workload restrictive? Is the norm in the work or the home situation the maintenance of old habits? Are there built-in time wasters in your lifestyle – travel, meetings, waiting for phone calls?

What are the obstacles in your world which you need to find strategies for?

By becoming more aware of what our most significant obstacles are we can be more appropriately selective about the strategies we identify to make a difference. We can also make better decisions about where to start.

If we believe that the most significant obstacles are in the system, and therefore beyond our control, we often give up because we don't think that we can change the system. However, if we can recognize that some of our obstacles are in ourselves we can certainly tackle those and begin to move towards our desired effectiveness. If some are caused by others we can look for strategies to influence them to respond differently and again make some steps towards our desired state.

Having achieved that, it is worth noticing that we will feel more in control and may find strategies to begin to make a difference to the system. Most systems are as they are because of people's tacit conspiracy to treat them as an abstract thing rather than as something created by and maintained by people.

Strategies for increasing time for development

If you want to improve your time management you will look for your own strategies in the variety of sources of useful information available, so we will not cover that ground here. There are, however, some particularly relevant NLP strategies which are worth mentioning as they may be useful to you.

Use of language

The way we describe things affects how we deal with them and how others interpret them as well. We can adjust our descriptions of time, and of our work, and thereby adjust the effect on us and others. If I tell myself there is always enough time and it's up to me to use it well, I establish in my own mind that I have control over what happens rather than being run by the clock.

When I describe myself as a trainer, I give myself and others the impression that the important part of my work is standing up and conveying information. When I describe myself as someone who models excellence in learning and facilitates the learning of others I begin to give equal importance to the preparatory and self-development aspects of my work. Then a half-day spent reading a new book on managing change is not 'spare time' reading which could be pushed aside for other things, but a vital part of my work.

When we plan our week and use different categories for our activities it becomes justifiably full, yet balanced. The categories might be:

- preparation of material;
- identification of opportunities;
- self-preparation;
- follow-up;
- implementation of training;
- reflection and learning;
- support work;
- updating;
- self-development;
- maintaining resourcefulness.

Notice how you describe what you fill your time with and how that affects your attitude and that of others, and make some changes if they would be useful to you.

The use of experience

Changing our description of our activities can help to begin to give us a different set of priorities in terms of how we use our time. We can enhance that effect by using our own best experiences as evidence. When we have been excellent in what we do, what has made the difference? If we compare best times to all right times, including what we did beforehand and what we did afterwards, we begin to notice the relative value of different uses of our time. The proposals contained in this book all spring from such comparisons, both in my own experience and that of others.

When we have evidence from our own experience that time spent on both self-development and self-resourcing has significant pay-offs in how we perform, then we will want to find time for those activities in our lives, and it is remarkable how we do find time for things we are motivated to do. We can also use our own experience to remind ourselves of times when we have been effective in our time management and notice what we did or thought that made a difference. These are always useful strategies as they are already customized to suit us.

Motivating yourself

A problem that most of us have is turning good ideas or intentions into action. It is one thing to know what you have to do, it is another to motivate yourself to do it.

None of us has only tasks which we genuinely want to tackle, and a frequent cause of time wasting or ineffective use of time is that we are putting off doing something that we don't want to do. We can tackle this in several ways with NLP techniques.

Commands to the unconscious

Instead of telling yourself that you ought to or must do x, try telling yourself that you will. We are unconsciously more responsive to 'will' than 'ought to', because 'will' is our choice whereas 'ought to' is externally imposed on us.

Change your focus

If that isn't enough, try changing your perspective on the task. We often focus on something we don't want to tackle to such an extent that we cannot see past it. What's more, it becomes bigger and more unattractive in our imaginations as we continue to pay attention to it.

By shifting our perception, we can bring it back into perspective. We can do this in two ways:

1. Tell yourself that you want it done, and remind yourself of the effect, on you and others, of having completed it.
2. Give yourself something to look forward to after you have completed this task. 'When I have completed this, I will go for a walk.'

Both shift your focus from the task itself to the positive after-effects – we can often be motivated to do things by the reward at the end, just as children are!

Changing your perception

As an alternative, you can regain perspective on the task you are avoiding by making it smaller, literally or metaphorically.

1. Break the task down into sections, and consider the completion of each section as an achievement. You can then plan the sections into your time, with other more attractive activities in between.
2. Imagine that the task is an object. Give it a shape, texture and colour in your mind. Now change that object into something smaller and more attractive by changing the shape, texture and colour. You will now find it easier to tackle.

Redefining avoidance

Most of us have a vast repertoire of avoidance strategies. Instead of using them as another reason to feel guilty and putting ourselves into an even less resourceful state for tackling the task, we can redefine them and make them useful.

A typical avoidance strategy is finding something else we have to do is suddenly more important than the task we can't face. If we redefine we may well get both tasks done well.

Instead of calling it avoidance, call it part of your preparation for the task you need to do. For example, 'Writing this letter is helping me to resource myself for the task'. By allowing ourselves to do the alternative without guilt, and by treating it as an example of our unconscious wisdom which prompts us to get ourselves into the right state of readiness first, we will usually find that we are ready for the task when we have finished the alternative.

Strategies for saving time

NLP also offers us some useful strategies which can enhance our effectiveness in using time so that we have more to spare for the other essential components of our excellence as trainers – development and relaxation time.

Being resourceful

A basic NLP principle is that the state we are in affects our performance. We all know that tasks can take more time or less time, depending on the mood we're in. It is useful, therefore, to take a little time before we begin anything to trigger ourselves into an appropriate state to tackle the task effectively. To achieve this we need to use the process already described:

- Remember a time when you were in that state or tackled a similar task effectively.
- Notice how you were physically and mentally.
- Choose a word or phrase, a visual image, or a physical repositioning to be the trigger for you to reproduce that state.

This trigger, when imagined in your head, will immediately reproduce for you the required state of resourcefulness to do the task more effectively.

It is also useful to remind ourselves that we need to give ourselves permission to take a break between intense activities. Even five minutes spent taking a walk outside or sitting with a cup of tea and an empty mind can be enough to let our brains relax and then gear up again for the next task.

Using our unconscious to do some of the work

We can save time on tasks we have to do by using our unconscious to do some of the work. We have all had the experience of being surprised at how much we seemed to have at our fingertips in a discussion or written piece of work which we hadn't consciously prepared for properly. We assume that we were just having an inspired moment.

In fact, this ability to use our unconscious rational mind is a great help in saving time. All it requires is that we instruct ourselves correctly, and we can use it to sort information, plan the order of things and word things correctly. For example:

1.   I have read a great deal of different information about research into leadership skills. I now want to identify key themes around which to construct a course. I tell myself, 'I want to list the key themes tomorrow morning', and I then leave that and do other things, deliberately distracting my conscious mind. The following morning I sit down at the word-processor, type the title 'Key themes on leadership skills' and ask myself, 'Now, what are the key themes?', and begin to input.
2.   Having identified the key themes, I want to put them into a suitable order for presenting them. I tell myself, 'I want these in an order which will make sense to my audience by the time I come back to this'. I then go away and again distract my conscious mind for an hour or two. When I return, I ask myself, 'What will be a useful order for these?', and just follow my intuition.

3.   I now need to script the presentation. Again, I instruct myself, 'I want to

express these themes in a way which makes sense to my audience'. I may add, 'And I want examples to make the themes relevant to their experience'. Again, after a period of conscious distraction, I come back to the word-processor and write the script 'off the top of my head'.

You may want to use just one part of this process rather than the whole. Or you may want to experiment with it only when you are struggling with something and your conscious mind is not succeeding in the task. We need to build our own evidence that it is an excellent way to save ourselves conscious thinking time and that it results in work which is at least as good as that which we produce by conscious thought.

Filtering for learning opportunities

Often we put off doing something about our own development because we perceive the amount of time we require as more than we want to spare. We have a mental image of development as something we have to think about, plan for and put a big chunk of time aside for. This is true of some development, but in the meantime we are often missing out on many opportunities which simply present themselves.

If we give our unconscious the command to notice learning opportunities we can make the most of these opportunities as they arise. Once we begin to notice these opportunities we find that they are there almost all the time.

- The simple question 'How else could I/they have tackled that?' gives us an extended repertoire very easily and quickly after any piece of training.
- The radio/TV programmes which may be relevant and useful seem to spring out on the page.
- The throw-away comment by a colleague about something different he or she has done or experienced is noticed and picked up.
- The article in the newspaper or journal draws our attention.

All these take little time, but add to our own development.

We have paid much attention to ways of ensuring that you have time for your own development because time, or lack of it, is expressed as an important obstacle to self-development. Take a moment or two now to consider which of these strategies you can and will use to increase the time available for you to develop your own abilities and skills. By making a commitment to yourself to take one or two simple steps to improve your time management you make it more likely that you will actually do something about it. So re-read this chapter quickly, and write down one or two first steps that you will begin to take tomorrow.

11 Methods of Self-development

Now that we have considered ways of creating more space for self-development, we should remind ourselves of the various ways we can use this space. In this chapter I will offer a broad description of ways of developing ourselves as well as a reminder of how we can enhance the learning process for ourselves.

Before we do this it is useful to remind ourselves of the purpose of self-development.

Purpose of self-development

Objective purpose of self-development as a trainer

There is a strong self-development thread running throughout this book. It is what we are encouraging others to do, so that we help organizations to set up a truly learning culture. We can provide an influential model for this, and this means being active learners ourselves. We also need to keep abreast of the rapidly changing world of organizations and of training, and can only do so by continuously looking for opportunities to find out.

Finally, we are facilitators of learning and development and we need to refine our skills continually in offering this service.

These are the factual reasons why we need to be engaged in continuous self-development. However, this objective purpose is not enough. If we are to commit ourselves fully to such development, we have to ensure that we are personally motivated rather than just intellectually convinced or, in some cases, professionally compelled to do it.

NLP proposes that we are all naturally good learners who have been put off when the way in which potential learning is presented to us becomes complex and appears difficult. This proposal is borne out by our own experience. When we are really motivated to learn something, and it is presented in a way which appeals to us, most of us revert to being good learners.

For example, there are classes full of voluntary adult learners who are enjoying learning foreign languages, particularly when the language is spoken in a place where they like to go on holiday. Of these, large numbers will declare that they were no good at languages at school. The difference is surely two-fold:

1. They can see some personal benefit for learning the language.
2. The approach is far more practical and useful to them.

NLP research has shown that excellent people all find some personal benefit in what they undertake, as a means of helping themselves to commit to whatever it is.

Similarly, our purpose for self-development has to give us some personal benefit if we are to be motivated to pursue it. And for each of us there will be different things which we see as making the effort worthwhile. So, defining my purpose in self-development will necessarily lead me to consider some of the potential personal benefits it might bring. Otherwise my commitment to it will never be wholehearted.

Potential benefits

For some of us the benefits which matter will be purely personal. Examples would be:

*   I enjoy learning new things.
*   I enjoy the challenge of new ideas.
*   I'm curious about what others are doing and thinking in my field.
*   I want to be ahead of the game.

Sometimes the benefits are in terms of how my self-development will affect others:

*   I will be recognized for my enhanced knowledge.
*   I will be a better model for my clients.
*   I will be able to provide even better training for others.

And sometimes the most motivating aspects will be to do with the professional rewards I can gain:

- I will be able to get a better job.
- I will be able to charge more for my services.
- I will be considered more valuable to my organization.

Most of us will have a mixture of these types of benefits which for us makes the package to which we respond. It is important to recognize these for ourselves, and to be honest about it. For example, I am much more committed to the personal gains than to those linked to professional reward, yet I like the fact that I become more valuable and valued when I engage in self-development. It is a useful by-product but not my most powerful motivator.

Take a few moments and write down what you would see as being the benefits to you of continuous self-development and then asterisk the ones which are most important for you. You now have a clearer picture of what will make your self-development seem worthwhile for you. You can also use this picture to help you to make sense of the objective purpose of any self-development by adding your personal benefits to the objective statement.

What self-development?

There are so many ways in which we can develop ourselves. It can be difficult to decide what to pursue, and we need to have some rationale for ourselves to make those decisions easier, otherwise we can spend half our potential development time wondering what to develop!

Most of us have learnt to make such decisions based on logical criteria: these are the areas I need to develop so these are the ones I will follow. Alternatively, we may fall into the category of those who follow a particular path of development because it happens to be available at this moment. Although this is something we are trying to move away from in the training of others, it is none the less often the way we and others make the choice.

When considering excellent people, it is interesting to notice how they make their choices for self-development.

Using every opportunity

The first difference is that those who are excellent treat everything as a potential learning opportunity. They seem to have a permanent question in their heads: 'What can I learn from this?' When they describe situations they have been in, they automatically talk about what they noticed, realized or had re-affirmed through the experience.

This may seem like a complicated way of perceiving the world, but in fact it matches the way we function naturally as children. To set up this mindset is easy. You simply tell yourself that you want to notice anything which will add to your learning, or that you want to have that question as a standard part of your normal way of perceiving things. You may not even notice what you are noticing consciously, and you will still gain the learning and development.

If you want to take it a stage further, you can use the simple review process I have described before. At the end of the day, just take a few moments to go through and review your day.

1. Identify something which you did well and notice what you did that made the difference. It may be something you said or some action you took, or just the way you were when you handled it.
2. Identify something you wish you had handled better. Now imagine that you have the chance to replay that scene. How would you do it differently, so as to get the desired effect? Play the revised version through in your head a couple more times.

You have now confirmed your own good practice, and created a better version of a piece you want to improve, and by running them through in your head you have increased the likelihood of repeating the best versions again in the future.

This takes up little of our time but it can significantly affect our development without much effort.

Specific self-development

When excellent people choose to pursue actively a specific area for their self-development they make their choice through a combination of their logical and their intuitive mind. By using a slightly more complex process of decision making they are able to ensure that the form of development they have chosen will be useful to them and will add to their development. This process is unconscious and may indeed be what prompts you in your choices. It is useful to spell it out consciously however, so that we can choose to use it when we are unsure of what we should do.

Process of selection

1. Identify potential areas for development by assessing present strengths and weaknesses.
2. Make sure that the areas you have selected for development are ones which you want and need to develop. There is often a sense that we ought to develop some particular skill, quality or behaviour, rather than a desire to do so. If this is the case, ask yourself, 'What would be the consequences of not developing in that area?', and, 'How else could I cater

for my lacks in that area?' You may find that it is not necessary for you to include this area in your development plan after all.

For example, you may think that you should develop your skills in producing graphics for your handouts. By asking yourself these questions, you may discover that it would be more useful to ask someone else who enjoys doing such things to do graphics for you while you concentrate on the areas you are comfortable with. You may still think you should learn to do it yourself, but at least now you are making that choice in a more informed way.

3. One other point is easily forgotten in the quest for development. Development means building on what we already have. It may be that we have absorbed the cultural tendency to consider only weaknesses as areas for development. It is worth examining your strengths and asking yourself if there are any of those areas which you would like to take further.

Excellent people do not consider any aspect of their development ever to be 'finished'. They are always looking for ways of enhancing what they already have.

Sometimes the most useful self-development you can undertake is the further development of an area you are good at.

4. Identify potential benefits to you of pursuing these areas of development. Remember that what motivates us to take action is being able to identify a gain which matters to us personally.

5. Now look at your list and select the area(s) which have most appeal for you. This is where you bring your intuition into the game. The area which is most appealing is likely to be the one where you will a) make the most difference and b) be committed to getting value out of the learning.

There is one further point to be made about this process. It sets us up to notice anything which might help us in our self-development so that we find the opportunities we need to further our own progress. This means that we have a yardstick against which to measure those opportunities which just happen to be available and are able to make a more informed decision about them. We don't even have to think hard about it or make conscious reference to our original checklist. For example, I have received three invitations to seminars in the last week. One of them I threw away instantly. I knew that it was not what I want at the moment. One I was tempted by. It seemed to fit logically with the development I need to do. However, a few minutes considering it led me to confirm the feeling that this was not the method I would respond to best or get the most out of. The third one didn't seem to have any particular relevance to my conscious awareness of my development needs, yet it continued to appeal to me. I have applied for that one, because my previous experience tells me that my unconscious wisdom knows best, and that I have gained a lot from those events which I have felt drawn to despite my logic telling me that they weren't relevant.

When we allow ourselves to be guided by our unconscious wisdom as well as our conscious logic we are likely to select our development far more successfully.

Methods of self-development

Point 5 above begins to look at the next stage of choosing development. Having selected what we want to develop, we can consider how we are going to develop it.

Selecting the right method

As trainers we know about the various ways in which we can develop and about their appropriateness for different forms of development. What we can add to that knowledge is the awareness of our own preferred channel of communication. Do you prefer to listen to someone telling you about something or reading it to yourself (auditory)? Do you prefer to see diagrams, examples, even the person while they are speaking (visual)? Or do you just want to try things out for yourself, experience the putting into practice (kinaesthetic)? Most of us are likely to prefer a personalized combination of these. What this checking out enables you to do is to identify what you need in any development you undertake.

Any speaker must be inspiring to hold my attention because I need an element of the kinaesthetic. So to be able to imagine myself doing what they are talking about, I need a speaker who is lively, tells stories and clearly lives it themselves. Similarly with books, I want to hear the author's voice and be convinced of their wholehearted commitment to what they are discussing so that I get the feel of what they are covering rather than just the facts.

As trainers, we should be more prepared than most to take control of our own learning and development. We know what makes the difference for us, and we want to use our time effectively. It is important to select methods which are most effective for us and which suit our particular development purpose.

Being clear about your outcomes

NLP's emphasis on setting clear outcomes is also relevant in helping us to select our methods of development. We need to stop and think what exactly we want out of this development.

Some examples may help. I may want some very specific development:

- I want to increase my knowledge base on this subject.
- I want to learn some new ways of doing this.
- I want some new examples of this.

Or I may want something less defined:

- I want to feel enthused about the subject again.
- I want to find out what others do.
- I want to check how my practice compares with the good practice being suggested.

As we stop to think about what we want out of this development we can imagine ourselves when we have it. How will I feel? What will I be saying? What will I be doing? This enhances our ability to choose appropriately, to meet our own outcomes.

Formal methods

It is important to take advantage of the formal opportunities for development available to us. We benefit from this in several ways:

- Workshops and seminars can give us the chance to enhance our own skills and knowledge base.
- We experience being a learner in a formal way again and are reminded of what it is like for our learners.
- We have the opportunity to experience how another trainer works and to use it to compare our own style and maybe add to our repertoire.

We will only gain these advantages if we remember that we are there to learn. We have the right of any learner to question the usefulness of the training being offered. When I was first in training my sympathy for the position of the trainer led me to inhibit my own reactions so as not to upset them. This doesn't help either me or the trainer. If the training is not meeting my needs the first thing I should do is to see if the trainer can respond differently. If it is clear that they will not be able to offer what I want I may look at what else I could gain from this training. For example, I have been in workshops which were not giving me the skills development I wanted yet I found it useful enough to observe another trainer's approach and to share experience with other participants to feel that it was worthwhile staying. On the other hand, I have been in seminars where I felt that I was not getting any value from the experience. In these cases, we both gain from my removing myself from the training, and I can do that in a respectful way.

With books, open learning and computer-based training, I am more in control. They can give me similar benefits, including the comparison with another trainer's style, in that they all represent another trainer's approach to communicating what they have to offer. They also give me the choice of timing, pace and level of involvement. With these forms of formal training it is much easier to use your discrimination as to whether it is really what you need – there is no obvious human being at the receiving end of your rejection.

The only block we need to be aware of is the voice inside us that says we should finish what we have started. For me this obligation is useful only if I have chosen to check this material for use with others. There are now so many different approaches to training and development on the market that we can choose to try something different to make learning easier for ourselves.

Informal methods

It is easy to discount the myriad ways in which we can gain self-development which are not formally labelled as training. If we are to give value to development in others through these informal paths we need to start by valuing them properly for ourselves. I have already talked about some of the ones which are easily built into our own training practice: use of feedback from participants; reflecting on our own practice; actively looking for new ways of approaching something when we are doing our preparation. As excellent trainers, we should already be doing these things, and we should also give credit to ourselves for doing so.

We can extend the value of this form of development by being explicit in our training about the areas where we are trying out something new and experimenting with different approaches. This will engage our learners in the process of development and lead to even more valuable feedback. It also models for them the importance of acknowledging that you are learning and demonstrates that it is safe, and indeed useful, to do so.

Learners are both sympathetic and very helpful in speeding up the development. I was once trying out a new approach to basic health and safety training which involved using a board-game. When I said that it was an experiment the group concerned took part enthusiastically and proceeded to give a level of feedback I had never experienced from them before. They pointed out what they felt was good about the game and then took those parts which they felt could be improved and gave me suggestions for how to make the improvements. At the next session I took the improved version along to show them and thanked them for their help. I also apologized for taking up so much of their time on this experiment, which I saw as being essentially for my immediate benefit. They said how much they had gained from being involved in the process – awareness of how such games could help learning, self-confidence from having suggestions taken seriously, recognition of the value of constructive feedback – and that being a learner was not something to be ashamed of. We ended up submitting this game as a joint venture to be published for use with other similar groups.

Professional co-operation

Besides using the opportunities already afforded to us by the nature of the work we do, we can choose to extend our informal learning by co-operating with our professional colleagues.

This may already be a part of what you do: sharing ideas, asking each other for help or inspiration, delighting in successes and sympathizing with less effective moments often takes place in coffee breaks and quiet times. We can take this a stage further by deliberately seeking out opportunities to talk about our work with colleagues and to ask about what they are doing.

We can extend it further into an agreed form of mutual development where we set time aside for such discussions and structure its use. This form of mutual support is very useful and can enhance the performance of the department as a whole, as well as being a good model for the learners, who will soon discover that the training department is yet again practising what it preaches on the subject of co-operation and learning from each other.

Even if you work alone most of the time you can still set up this sort of arrangement with fellow professionals. You are likely to know other people involved in the same line of work and can engage them in this form of development. If you feel that you do not have the contacts you need, then looking for suitable candidates can give membership of professional organizations added value.

By sharing with other trainers in this way we can streamline some of our own development. I know that there are some who share a love of books and will let me know if there is something I should read, and I will do the same for them. There are other colleagues with whom I find it particularly useful to sound new ideas out or who will come up with some useful ideas when something I am doing isn't working and I don't know what to try next. Sometimes colleagues just provide the support and encouragement I need to experiment and sometimes they can indicate a good way of developing a particular area.

By actively developing this network with other professionals we can help each other to develop our skills and qualities. As we become more comfortable in relating to each other as fellow learners it is also possible to have the added value of being able to observe each other at work. By sitting in on other people's training we can discover different ways of handling situations and subjects. We can also give them a different quality of feedback because of our awareness of the training role. This means that the activity has mutual benefit.

We know that people learning together will tend to get more out of it than those who are tackling something on their own. It is another area where we can really extend our own good practice while still controlling the learning by making our own choices of with whom we co-operate and how.

Models

One further form of self-development which is worth mentioning specifically is the use of models of good practice. I have already referred to this form of learning. There are the obvious models of good practice for us as trainers – other trainers who are putting into practice the skills or qualities which we want to develop. Simply by spending time with them we begin to absorb the ways in which they enable themselves to make the difference. And, of course, we can ask them questions to discover what exactly they think and do to achieve the effect we want to emulate.

There are, however, other models, outside the field of training, who can be very useful to us. There are managers who handle difficult staff very well, there are shopkeepers who establish rapport quickly and effectively with their customers, there are communicators in many fields who get their message across effectively. They are all potential sources of development for me, and give me an excellent reason to pursue other interests and activities while continuing to learn.

Leading edge

Remember that we work in a field where rapid development is taking place. When selecting our methods of development we should consider how we can keep up to date with the latest ideas. Professional journals can be very useful for this. A quick skim through the latest arrival can tell you if there is anything new which you might want to pursue. Book and multi-media reviews can give a clue about important new material available. There is also increasing use being made of computer-based information updates. Are you on the Internet yet?

Personal development

There is one final point on self-development. As well as constantly looking for ways of improving our skills as trainers, we should maintain the round-edness of our development. If we are practising what we are preaching we will be engaging in development which is not directly related to our work. An important factor in my effectiveness in my work is my enthusiasm and *joie de vivre*. This is maintained by continuing to enrich my life experience so that I am a whole person, not just a trainer.

Whether it be through learning a new sports activity, or beginning to learn about photography, or exploring a country we have never visited before, we need to ensure that we are catering for the whole person as we develop ourselves. And at the same time we are giving ourselves the opportunity to notice things which we could transfer into our work, as well as giving ourselves the space to keep a healthy perspective on what we do in our work.

As you were reading through this chapter you probably said to yourself that it is mostly common sense, that you are constantly promoting these messages about self-development to others. But we still welcome the reminder that we need to practise what we preach to be at our best.

You may do many of these things without calling them self-development. Yet we need to recognize and value these activities so that they are seen as valuable uses of our time. Our ability to be excellent trainers is directly linked to our own continuous learning and development.

Part V

Activities

Throughout this book I have used NLP type activities to help you in developing your excellence as a trainer. From the experience of applying the principles and techniques of NLP to your own development you will be able to use NLP activities more effectively with your own learners. Whenever you use NLP with others, remember to:

- ensure that you have established rapport;
- check the ecology – is it right for them?;
- remind them that these techniques are already a part of their unconscious repertoire;
- pay full attention to how they are responding and notice if you need to change tack;
- link the activity directly to their own experience and the area you are looking at.

By remembering to ensure that you have covered all the common threads which run throughout NLP activities you will bring added value to any you use with others.

This part will provide the basis of a repertoire which employs this approach to develop excellence in your training. I will give descriptions of activities you have already used in your own development, and how, with suitable adaptation, they can be applied with your learners. I will also add some more activities to the repertoire, with suggestions of where they may be helpful in a training context.

I have selected activities which can easily be adapted for use with individuals or with groups. I have also chosen ones which can be helpful in a variety of learning contexts, formal and informal, so that you can employ them to facilitate learning wherever and whenever there is an opportunity.

The activities listed here are ones which you can label 'different' rather than 'NLP.' I have used them with people who would not be prepared to do something they regarded as esoteric, making clear the fact that they are similar to ways we approach situations in our everyday lives, just a bit more conscious. Those who wish to 'do NLP' will pursue particular trainings in it. For most of us NLP needs to be translated back into something more accessible and recognizable, to be useful.

Activity 1   Reviewing Beliefs and Values

I have already described how this activity can help you as a trainer to develop the personal qualities which support excellence. It can equally well be employed in any situation where there may be limiting beliefs which inhibit development. For example, I have used it on managing change programmes and when coaching managers in interpersonal skills.

The Activity

Ask the group or individual to make themselves comfortable and enjoy the chance to reflect on themselves.

Point out that we are used to reviewing our beliefs about ourselves and others, although we wouldn't normally call it that. Our tendency is to notice what we don't think we can do or how we don't think we can be. When we don't succeed at something we tend to notice all the times we haven't succeeded in the past, and thereby confirm for ourselves our belief that we are not good at something. This process is designed to put us in a state where we can counteract those negative or limiting beliefs we hold by allowing us to notice a different set of evidence from our experience.

Talk the learner through this process, taking one stage at a time. If you are working with a group you may choose to ask them to create the checklists as small groups.

Reviewing beliefs about yourself

1. Identify what you would say are the qualities of someone who is excellent at this particular skill – what is he or she like, what can he or she do?

169

2. Go through the list and tick all the qualities which you believe you already have.
3. Check through those which you have not yet ticked. Give yourself credit for having some degree of the quality, if that is true, even if it is not as consistent as you would like. (Give the group some examples of where we might have demonstrated this quality or skill in a different context so they have some clues about how to look beyond their normal frames of reference.)
4. Search through your personal history, consciously looking for examples of where you may have demonstrated any qualities still remaining unticked. These examples may come from any sphere or period of your life.
5. Now take those which you have ticked and restate them as affirmations. Begin them with either 'I can' or 'I am'. Read them all out slowly to yourself.

Reviewing beliefs about others

1. What, in this context, would be a useful set of beliefs for you to hold about others? Compile your own checklist.
2. Go through your list and tick those which you already have as beliefs.
3. Go through again and search through your experience for examples to begin to support some of the statements you haven't yet ticked. Remember to use any context – it doesn't matter where your examples come from.
4. You may still have some statements about others for which you can find no support, but by now most items on your list should be evidenced, at least to some degree.
5. We now need to embed these beliefs into your unconscious as your expectations of others.

   - Begin with those you already hold, and reaffirm them by writing them down again, and saying them out loud, remembering, at the same time, examples of evidence.
   - Take the second set, where you eventually thought of examples, and express them as possibilities: 'People can decide for themselves the best way of doing something'.
   - As you write them down, think again of your example.
   - Take the third set, which is any statements for which you couldn't find supporting evidence, and express them as: 'I want to believe that people ... '.
   - As you write them down, imagine how someone would react in a particular situation if they were like that.

Reviewing beliefs about how the world works

Begin by explaining what this means. You may choose to use a couple of examples which are common sayings in your culture, for example: 'pride comes before a fall' or 'there's no gain without pain'. Point out how powerfully they can affect what we think is possible.

1. Create a list of core beliefs about how the world works which would be useful to you in this context.
2. Now, as before, go through the list ticking those you already hold as beliefs.
3. Go through a second time, consciously looking for any evidence in your experience that would support any unticked beliefs.
4. Embed these beliefs in your unconscious. Take all those you have some evidence for and rewrite them as 'I believe ...' statements, saying each one out loud and thinking as you do so of your evidence.
5. Now write the rest down as 'I want to believe ...' statements, and when you say each one out loud, add: 'and I will begin to look for supporting evidence from now on'.

Activity 2   Eliciting a Positive State

I have described how this activity can be used to help you as a trainer, and to help learners to be in an excellent learning state and feel that what they are about to do is within their realms of possibility.

It can also be employed as part of the development of their skills to make them realize that they can prepare themselves by this method to perform well in whatever context you are training in. For example, I may use it in counselling training or in preparation for an interview.

Further, it reminds the learner that they can have control over their state and is thus another way of developing their personal empowerment. Most people recognize that it provides them with a tool that they can use to help themselves be ready for any situation where they want to be at their best.

The Activity

Make sure that your group or individual are sitting comfortably and are in a relaxed state. Then talk through the process with them slowly and with a gentle tone of voice.

Explain to them at the start that we all unconsciously adopt a certain physical position, tone of voice and mental state when we go into any particular state. Give them a couple of examples which they might have experienced, such as when the boss asks to see them – a negative example for most people – or when someone asks about a good holiday they have just had.

Although the physical and mental state we are in affects quite dramatically the way we then behave, most of the time we are unaware of it and so do nothing to change it. This activity helps them to become aware so that they can adjust themselves to produce their best when they want to.

173

Process for creating an excellent state

1.   Define the state you want to be able to re-create. Express that state in your own words, for example; 'feeling confident'.
2.   Remember a time, a specific example, when you did demonstrate this quality. It doesn't matter what the context was, or how long you were like this for. Accept any example your mind comes up with even if you're not sure it's the best one. Our minds are very good at finding appropriate examples for this activity, even if they are not the ones we would consciously select.
3.   Now allow yourself to go back into that moment of excellence. Remember the setting, the others involved, and go and relive the moment.
4.   As you go back into the moment fully, begin to notice information about yourself in that state – and if you're not sure you can remember the information accurately, imagine what it would be. First, notice anything you can see there which draws your attention – or that you don't notice anything in particular.
5.   Now notice anything you can hear in that situation – or that you don't hear anything much.
6.   How does it feel to be demonstrating this quality well? Notice where you feel the satisfaction, what sensations you have.
7.   Pay more attention to your actual physical state. Are you mobile or still? Which muscles in your limbs, your torso, your shoulders, are tense and which relaxed? Notice what makes you physically comfortable when demonstrating this quality and whether there is any particular posture or gesture associated with it.
8.   Examine your facial expression, how it changes and stays the same as you demonstrate this quality. Notice if your jaw is clenched, what your eyes are like, and if your head is on one side or straight on your body. Notice how you speak – tone and speed and loudness.
9.   Now go inside yourself and notice how you are breathing – fast or slow, deeply or shallowly.
10.   And what goes on inside your head when you're demonstrating this quality? Do you picture anything in your imagination or is the internal video screen empty? Do you say anything to yourself, or is the internal tape recorder silent? This is the type of information which you unconsciously collect in any situation. You then need to process it.
11.   Staying in that situation where you are demonstrating the quality you want to re-create, allow all the information you have collected to filter down through your consciousness and then ask yourself:

   ●   What could I picture to myself that would instantly remind me of this state?

- What could I say to myself that would instantly remind me of this state?

Allow answers to spring to mind, and don't judge them – they may or may not be the logical conscious choice you would make. Triggers are frequently illogical, and we are creating triggers here.

12. Come back to the present and confirm to yourself these two triggers which will enable you to re-create the whole state, by saying to yourself: 'From now on, whenever I picture *x*, or say *y* to myself, I will automatically regain the physical, mental and emotional state I have when demonstrating this (quality) excellently.' You may like to record your triggers to reinforce the reminder.

This process can now be repeated with each of the qualities you wish to develop further so that you have a set of triggers for creating the appropriate state.

Sometimes we may wish to do this in a less formalized way. The following gives you an alternative approach.

Ask people to talk about times when they have performed well, in whatever context. For example, someone may feel that they were confident in tackling a new task in a domestic situation rather than a work situation – it still works as an example. If you have a group, then ask them to do this in small groups. If it is an individual, then you talk with them.

Start with a general description of the situation and what happened – already they will begin to take on the state they had when they were successful. Then ask them to notice specifically how they were physically when they were performing, what was going on in their heads, what their facial expression was like.

Now ask them to choose something which would remind them of this state – a word, a visual, a gesture. Tell them that it doesn't have to have an obvious rational link to the state – whatever first springs to mind will be useful. This is now their trigger to remind themselves instantly to take on this state. Whenever they think of this trigger they will instantly adopt the useful state again, physically and mentally.

Activity 3   Setting Outcomes

The ability to set full and clear outcomes is considered by NLP to be a pre-requisite in any situation. I have talked about this earlier in the book, particularly in the chapter on training preparation. Here I will give two versions of helping people to enhance their outcome setting which can be used in almost any training. For example, I have used it in training for consultancy skills and when coaching someone for a presentation.

The Activity

Version 1

1. Ask the participants to identify what they want as their outcome for this particular area. Stress that the outcome is the result which would make them feel they had been successful.
2. Help them to define that outcome more fully by answering the following questions:

    - What would you be doing and saying?
    - How would you be feeling?
    - What would others involved be doing and saying?
    - What other differences would you notice immediately?
    - What differences would you notice longer-term?

3. Point out that they have not only defined the outcome they want, they have also begun to clarify the evidence they need to tell them that their action has been successful.
4. Ask them to imagine themselves at the point of knowing that they have

177

successfully achieved their outcome, really feeling as if they have done it. Tell them that if they can imagine it, then it is possible.

Version 2

1. Ask the participants to imagine the best possible outcome for the particular situation. Tell them to act as if they have already achieved it, at the moment when they realize they have successfully fulfilled what they want.
2. Ask them to notice how they know they have been successful – what are they using as evidence? Take them through the same questions as for Version 1, only worded in the present.
3. Tell them to now state clearly to themselves the full outcome they want in this situation.

Activity 4   Improving Performance

This activity helps your learners to prepare for putting their learning into the work situation. It also gives them a chance to check that what they think will work will actually make the difference. Further, if there are any obstacles which will appear when they try to apply their learning they will show up at this stage and can be dealt with in readiness for the real situation.

The activity can be linked to the previous activity on outcomes to provide a full rehearsal of a future event and to give added value. It can also be used either with individuals or with a whole group, in which case you will take them through it in stages.

The Activity

Ask the learners to imagine the next work situation which will be coming up where they will have a use for the skills area which they have been developing. Tell them to visualize themselves acting out their part as they would normally, as if they were watching a video on a screen and hearing the dialogue or commentary.

Now ask them to be the director of this video and to treat this version as a rehearsal. What advice would they give to the actor about their script, their actions, their behaviour, to improve the performance?

Ask them to replay the video incorporating the improvements they have suggested, then to check this version to see if there is anything further they can suggest which would further enhance the performance.

Suggest they play the final version through to check that they are happy with it. Next, they imagine themselves moving into the actor and becoming him or her, performing the part perfectly. Then ask them to imagine that happening a second time.

They now know that they have woken up the circuitry in their brain to repeat this performance whenever they want to, by rehearsing it.

Activity 5   Using Wisdom with Hindsight Beforehand

This activity gives learners information about unconscious differences they can make to improve their performance in a given situation in addition to the obvious conscious, rational preparation and behaviour. It allows them to identify beforehand how they can put their learning into practice effectively and teaches them to use their intuitive wisdom. It links in with the activity on setting outcomes and gives them more information. It is particularly appropriate for using with someone when they are worried about applying the skills they have learnt to a future project.

The Activity

Point out that we all have two well-developed skills: the ability to have wisdom with hindsight, and the ability to predict scenarios. Our wisdom with hindsight is too late to make a difference to what happens and we frequently use our predictive ability to predict worst-case scenarios – and are usually accurate! This activity puts those two skills together to make them both more useful.

Ask your learners to think of a situation where they would like to improve their performance. Now ask them to imagine the best possible outcome to this situation. Go through the detail of the outcome. What would they be hearing? What would they be seeing? How would others be behaving? How would they be behaving? How would they be feeling? Get them to act as if they are at that moment of knowing that it has worked out exactly how they would want it to.

Point out that they have been simply predicting, but this time, predicting the best-case scenario. Now ask them to use their wisdom with hindsight.

While staying in the state of being at the successful outcome, ask them to answer some or all of the following questions to themselves:

- What helped you to achieve this outcome? And what else?
- How did you prepare yourself to achieve this outcome?
- What made the most difference to your achieving this outcome?
- What was the first step you took which led to this outcome?
- What state did you adopt to help you achieve this outcome?
- What resources supported you in achieving this outcome?

The answers to these questions will give you the extra information you need to make this outcome a reality. They come from your own intuitive wisdom and will work for you.

Activity 6   Checking Assumptions

In the chapter on preparation for training I referred to the importance for us as trainers of checking our assumptions. Of course this applies not only to us but also to everyone who is dealing with other people.

This activity points out the danger of getting the wrong message and helps people to see how they can clarify information they are being given. It is particularly useful in problem-solving activities where people often rush in with a solution before they have properly checked out what the problem really is.

The Activity

Point out that we frequently misinterpret what others mean by what they say, and that it is useful to check before we respond. Give an example, such as; 'When someone says that they can't do something, they may mean they haven't time; or they don't know how; or they don't want to; or it offends them in some way; or that they don't have any of the equipment needed.' We need to find out which of all the possible interpretations is accurate before we respond. By using simple questions we can ensure that our response is appropriate and we also make the person feel that we have paid attention to them and understood them.

Give out the Vague statements list (see p. 184) and write the questions on flip-chart. The aim of the exercise is to give learners practice in checking assumptions. They work in pairs, taking turns at reading out a statement and asking for clarification of meaning. (If you are doing this with an individual you will act as their partner.) Obviously, the person reading the statement will have to decide on their own interpretation.

You can draw up your own list of statements if you prefer to customize them for the particular group or situation.

183

Vague Statements

Unspecified nouns
Management doesn't let us do that.
We've developed a *policy* on that.
There are *rules* on that.
People demand *attention* all the time.

Unspecified verbs
We *use* guidelines to make decisions.
Planning your priorities *doesn't work.*
I won't be able to fit that in this week.
The staff *are involved in* deciding policy.

Rules
We *have to* complete the procedure at the time.
I *must* finish this job.
I *ought to* get back to the office by three o'clock.
You *shouldn't* assume that clients know what they want.

Generalizations
All mistakes are proof of lack of foresight.
They *always* change their minds.
None of my colleagues get it right.
Meetings are a waste of time.

General examples
The bosses said that we had to do it this way.
Discipline must be maintained in any organization.
That won't work in practice, although it's quite interesting.
The regulations always cause problems.

Reproduced from *The Excellent Trainer* by Di Kamp, Gower, Aldershot

The questions

For unspecified nouns
What exactly, who exactly, which exactly . . . ?
Can you give me an example of . . . ?

For unspecified verbs
How exactly, in what way exactly . . . ?
Can you give me an example of how . . . ?

For rules:
Who/what says that you . . . ?
What would happen if you did/didn't . . . ?

For generalizations
Are there any exceptions, can you think of any exceptions to this . . . ?
Which ones specifically do you notice this in . . . ?

Reproduced from *The Excellent Trainer* by Di Kamp, Gower, Aldershot

Activity 7 Gaining Perspective

In the chapter on preparation of training I talked about how important it is for us to be aware of the learner's perspective when planning the training. It is equally important in many other situations to be able to look at things from the other person's point of view and to be able to take an objective viewpoint.

I use this activity to get people to recognize the different viewpoints. I find it particularly useful when dealing with difficult interpersonal situations. If you are working with an individual you will have to talk them through each of the perspectives, as in the example in Chapter 7.

The Activity

Ask the learners to each think of a situation with another person where they feel that the other person is being an 'awkward customer'. It doesn't matter what the circumstances are, although you may choose to relate it to the specific context you are working on with them.

Ask them to form groups of three, and decide on initial roles – each of them will have an opportunity to take their issue through the activity. The roles are: the individual with the problem; the other they find hard to handle; an objective bystander.

Explain that the person with the issue will briefly outline the typical scenario and will demonstrate how the other reacts. This is important – they must show the others typical body posture and use typical tone of voice so that the others can play the part too. Point out that they do not have to give too much detail on the content. It doesn't matter if the content varies from what they have commonly experienced with this person – they are just using it as a starting-point.

Now ask the person with the issue to be their 'awkward customer', a second in the group to try to handle the situation in their role, and the third to observe. Play the situation for five minutes and then ask them to feed back to each other what they noticed from the different perspectives.

Now ask them to swap the roles: the person with the issue becomes the observer, the person playing their part becomes the 'awkward customer', and the person who observed takes the part of the person who found the situation difficult. Again let it run for five minutes, and then ask them to feed back what they noticed from the different perspectives.

Complete this round by asking them to take on the role they have not yet tried and repeat the process.

Now ask the originator to tell the others what they have learnt about dealing with their 'awkward customer' and what they will do differently next time they are in that situation.

Repeat the process for the issues of the other two group members.

Finish by asking the learners to form larger groups and identify what they have learned about dealing with people they find difficult. Feed that back and discuss in the whole group.

Activity 8   Levels of Attention

I have described this activity in detail in the section on implementing training. It is as useful for learners as it is for us as trainers. It reminds learners to notice the other signals which a person is giving in communication and to act on them rather than just the content. It also enhances the relationships within the group as they listen to each other without judgement. It is particularly useful in training on communication.

The Activity

Talk to the group about the purpose of the activity. You might say something like, 'The attention levels we commonly use give us only limited information. We may pick up factual information – what people say – and some very obvious non-verbal information such as if someone is consistently looking away, but we miss at the conscious level the small clues which can help us to adjust what we are doing before it reaches crisis point.'

Suggest that when we are paying attention, we need to use our whole selves:

- our ears – to hear the conscious message being given;
- our 'inner' ear – to hear the hesitations, enthusiasms, hidden questions;
- our eyes – to notice whether the body language matches the verbal message;
- our guts – to pick up those messages that are less obviously expressed;
- our hearts – to ensure that we respect and appreciate their viewpoint and use messages we pick up sympathetically.

Ask the group to form into pairs, so that they are all working with someone they don't know very well. Tell them that they are going to tell each other a story from their lives. It can be about anything so long as it has some significance for them: a holiday; a particular moment at work; a family or social event.

Give them a chance to choose who will talk first and then repeat the instructions for switching on full attention. Then suggest that they just enjoy the process of entering into someone else's world for five minutes. Make it clear that this is not a memory test – they are not going to be expected to repeat the story afterwards.

After five minutes ask them to stop, and ask the person who has been paying attention to tell the storyteller something they like about them.

Now repeat the process with a change of roles.

If you are using this with an individual you act as their partner.

Activity 9 Increasing Awareness of the Power of Language

This activity illustrates the effect language has on us, a theme which has recurred throughout this book. It will help learners to realize how they are affected by the way people express things to them, and teach them to counteract any negative effects.

It can be applied in any training context and is particularly apposite in a session on communication. If you use it with an individual you need to work with them to come up with their examples and alternatives.

The Activity

Ask people to identify words and phrases which have a negative effect on them. Give them a couple of examples: 'You're stupid' or 'Haven't you finished yet?'. Point out that these types of phrase make us feel demotivated and are unlikely to bring out our best performances.

When they have identified their own disempowering words and phrases, ask the learners to look at how they could change them to have a more useful effect, or how they could respond to them differently. Give examples such as; 'I haven't yet got this bit through to you' and 'How far have you got?' or, as different responses to the two statements; ' Yes, I haven't grasped this yet' or 'No, I'm putting a lot of care into it'.

Ask them to record their own changes to the words or phrases that they find disempowering.

Now ask them to identify some words or phrases which they find encouraging and empowering. Ask them for as many as they can think of and suggest that they use them as often as possible when describing things to themselves and others and monitor the effect.

Activity 10 Useful Questions

I have suggested different questions throughout this book. In my experience the questions which NLP has identified are one of the most useful tools. They can be used in two ways:

- as the questions you ask as trainer when facilitating learning;
- as a specific activity where you encourage the learners to practise using these questions instead of their usual ones.

I use them as an activity *per se* when dealing with people who need to find out information and to solve problems with others, such as consultants and managers.

The Activity

Ask the learners to think of a 'niggle' they have – something which bothers them but which is not so important that they have done something about it. I usually give examples, such as never getting round to filing things away, or the phone always ringing at the wrong moment.

Then ask them to form pairs. One is to tell the other about their niggle and the other can ask questions only from the useful questions list on p. 194. Emphasize that they cannot offer solutions and that they can use any of the questions in any order. Where you are working with an individual you will act as the partner and take first turn at asking questions as a demonstration.

Give the pairs five minutes to play each of the roles and then ask them to discuss what they have realized as a result of doing this activity.

Useful questions

Useful questions to elicit information
Use these to find out more about the issue from the point of view of the other person and to check your own assumptions:

What, how exactly . . . ?
Can you give me an example of . . . ?
What is important to you about . . . ?
What appeals to you about . . . ?
How do you know that . . . works?
What outcomes/results do you want?
What effect do you want?
What changes do you want?

Useful questions to encourage consideration of something
These questions help you to structure your own thinking about the issue and to produce solutions which will work for you.

What alternatives have you considered?
What would make it possible for you to . . . ?
How would you deal with . . . ?
What would make a difference to . . . ?
What would make it acceptable/worthwhile for you to . . . ?
How do you see this being resolved?
How could you change . . . ?

Useful questions to turn thought into action
Use these questions to help someone to identify what they are going to do as a result of thinking through their issue.

How could you begin to use . . . ?
What will be the first step?
How exactly can I/we help?
What are you now going to do?

Useful questions to extend possibilities
These questions should be used in conjunction with the ones above to help people think of alternative strategies so that they always have choices.

And what else . . . ?
And how else . . . ?

Activity 11 Using Metaphors

As a means of communicating, metaphors are very powerful. When people need to explain something to others they can enrich their explanation by using a metaphor. It is important to make clear that a metaphor can be created from a simple statement and is actually a common way of making sense of something for others.

I have used this activity to help people to define their work, their role, the vision of the team – almost anything where they are not able to capture the spirit of it in purely factual terms.

The Activity

Ask the group to suggest possible metaphors which would capture the spirit of what they are trying to express. It is useful to give a few relevant examples, such as, 'Some teams have described themselves as a sports team, others have said that they want to be like a commune. What do you want to be like, as a team?'

If you are working with an individual, you might say, 'Some people say that their job is like a circus, some would say that it is like drawing up a route map. How would you describe your job, what does it resemble that your client might be able to relate to?

Once the group has suggested an agreed metaphor, ask them to fill in some more detail:

- What does this say about how they act?
- What does it say about the prevailing atmosphere?
- What does it suggest about the way things work?

No doubt you will think of appropriate questions to help them to do this.

In some instances the development of the theme of the metaphor is enough to help learners to convey their message more effectively, for example as a way of describing their present role.

If you use it to help people to identify how they would like things to be, for example when defining a vision for a team or a goal for an individual, you can take the activity a stage further. Now that they have a clearer picture of the outcome they want and the effects it will have, how can they begin to work towards it?

You can simply ask them to work on this theme, or you can use the Wisdom with Hindsight Beforehand activity (pp. 181–2) to help.

You may like to explore the use of metaphors in more detail. In this case it is useful to begin by starting people's brains working on how metaphors are created. A simple approach to this is to give them a chance to play with making up metaphors by giving them a set of words to express metaphorically: 'work is like ...', 'learning is like ...', 'being a boss is like ...', and so on. This can be an enjoyable exercise and will illustrate the power of metaphor as well as how simple a metaphor can be.

You can then go on to ask the group to think of how they could use a metaphorical story to respond to someone in a variety of circumstances. Give an example, such as:

> When someone tells me that they are useless at something I usually tell them about the boy at the school where I used to teach. Darren was no good at anything and didn't even try any more. He had been told so often that he was stupid that he knew it was true. He seemed to pay no attention in any of his lessons, and said very little.
>
> One day I caught him playing with some bits of feathers and wire. When I asked him what he was doing he told me that he was making a fly for fishing. It turned out that this 'stupid boy' was an expert fisherman as well as an expert fly-maker. He could talk eloquently and knowledgeably about his subject and had skills and awareness that were beyond me.
>
> This boy's confidence grew when he realized that this meant that he wasn't stupid all the way through! He eventually became a skilled engineer, using skills and abilities which started with being interested in fishing.

Ask the group to identify situations where they would find it useful to have a story to tell so that they would convey what they wanted to say in a different way. Examples might be: when someone has said something critical or hurtful; when someone is finding life hard; when someone can't make up their mind. You might give them ones to work on or you may choose to ask them to identify their own.

If you are working with a group it can be useful to ask them to think up stories together in small groups, as they can then feed off each others' ideas. Tell them that the stories can be from real life or may be created for the purpose.

Ask them to tell their stories when they have finished and give them a chance to comment helpfully on each other's stories.

From these preliminary activities on metaphors you can go on to apply the use of metaphors in their work situation.

Recommended Reading

There are many books both on training methods and NLP. The following are those which I feel are the simplest and most useful for a trainer to adapt for their own work.

Covey, S.R. (1992), *The Seven Habits of Highly Effective People*, London: Simon & Schuster.
Although not strictly about training or NLP, this book contains valuable ideas about how to encourage the development of integrity in an accessible way.

Laborde, G.Z. (1987), *Influencing with Integrity*, Palo Alto, CA: Syntony Publishing.
An excellent description of the use of NLP techniques in communication, with clear examples and useful checklists.

McMaster, M. and Grinder, J. (1980), *Precision*, Bonny Doon, CA: Precision Models.
A very detailed description of how to improve your communication in order to elicit the information you want. It includes transcripts which illustrate how to apply the techniques.

O'Connor, J. and Seymour, J. (1994), *Training with NLP*, London: Thorsons.
A different description of applying NLP to training which will enrich your repertoire.

Robbins, A. (1988), *Unlimited Power*, London: Simon & Schuster.

Robbins, A. (1992), *Awaken the Giant Within*, London: Simon & Schuster.
Together these two books comprise an excellent introduction to the power of NLP techniques, with many examples and activities which you can use. One of the simpler expositions of NLP.

Russell, P. (1979), *The Brain Book,* London: Routledge & Kegan Paul.
An interesting and useful book on using your brain more effectively which complements much of the NLP material.

I would also recommend using audio-tapes and live training sessions to extend your NLP skills. It is very much an experiential discipline and makes a much greater impact through live experience.

I have produced a set of audio-tapes, 'The Dynamics of Excellence' which give a good introduction to the subject.

Index